D0890844

FOOTBALL

cancer life death

MICHAEL HEINICKE

FOOTBALL cancer life death

An uplifting story of one Burnley fan's
personal battle amid promotion

First published by Pitch Publishing, 2019

Pitch Publishing
A2 Yeoman Gate
Yeoman Way
Worthing
Sussex
BN13 3QZ
www.pitchpublishing.co.uk
info@pitchpublishing.co.uk

© 2019, Michael Heinicke

Every effort has been made to trace the copyright.
Any oversight will be rectified in future editions at the
earliest opportunity by the publisher.

All rights reserved. No part of this book may be reproduced,
sold or utilised in any form or transmitted in any form or by
any means, electronic or mechanical, including photocopying,
recording or by any information storage and retrieval system,
without prior permission in writing from the Publisher.

A CIP catalogue record is available for this book
from the British Library.

ISBN 978 1 78531 528 2

Typesetting and origination by Pitch Publishing
Printed and bound in India by Replika Press Pvt. Ltd.

Contents

Part One
TODAY

Saturday 21 February 2015

Today's the day then. Today's the day we finally get a win.

The North Down & Ards Small Sided Games Programme for the 2007 age group started back in September of last year and the team I coach, Ards FC Academy, are still yet to win a game. There's been 15 rounds of fixtures; 15 defeats in a row. Well, more than that actually. I even entered a second team after Christmas to double my chances, but it still hasn't happened for us. Instead of losing once a week, I'm losing twice a week. Not that it's about winning at this age – obviously. These boys are only seven and eight. Winning is a dirty word, except when you can't get a win. Then you need one. That's when it becomes about winning.

My first stop this morning is the new 3G pitch at Spafield for a 9am kick-off against Holywood. The section at Spafield is 2007/08 kids so the standard isn't as good. But we still haven't been able to buy a win up there. At least we've scored a couple though and we're not quite getting hammered by as many. All depends where you're starting from, doesn't it? I have come to learn that there is such a thing as a good hammering – I'd rather get beat by 5-1 than 15-0.

15-0 is no exaggeration. One of the early games in the 2007 section in Bangor, we were playing Ards Rangers in a local derby (they're all local but this one especially) and we got absolutely battered. It was horrible.

We received our first parent complaint that week. That was nice of them. Apparently, me and my coach, Phil, 'did nothing', we just 'watched and let it happen'. It's five-a-side and seven-year-olds, what are they expecting? Do they think that we can do something, like, tactically? Tinker with it? Christ on a bike, I can't talk tactics with kids who can't even tie a bootlace.

There's two reasons why we got hammered. Firstly, the kids we played against were stronger physically – my lot are on the young side and lack power and pace. But the bigger issue is that the other kids are better at football – they've better ball control, they can dribble, shoot, and some of them can even pass. We barely got a kick. How they want me and Phil to instantly address that minor issue on a Saturday morning when we're 8-0 down I've no idea, but it's not something easily fixed.

I can explain it a bit as well. Most of my group are quite new to football. A lot of them only joined this season. A few that had been down last year, well, they didn't really have anybody to coach them, they were just passed around a wee bit, so they're all lacking practice. Nobody owned them until now. But now they're mine and I'm accountable and responsible. It takes time. Other teams in the same age group have been up and running for a year or two. They're years ahead, which when you're only seven is a long time.

I'm patient with this. My own kids aren't involved with the club. I've no conflicts of interest. It's easy for me. It's all about development. I rotate the players, giving everybody a fair chance, regardless of ability. I want to develop them. All of them. So I'm fine with losing games if I've stuck to my principles. I make substitutions when I know that by doing so I'm potentially throwing the game.

And we do lose. Every single game.

Keep going though, we can turn this corner, climb this mountain. We're getting better and that's what matters. Not winning, that doesn't matter. But winning is a barometer for measuring that we've got better. I want to measure up. I want to win. Just once, one win. Monkey off the back. Put it to bed. And then we can kick on.

Today. It has to be the day. Let's win, boys.

I pull up at Spafield on my own and make my way down to the pitch. Even before we kick off I've a good feeling here – our opponents look similar to us physically – for once. Still, we start as slow as ever and go a goal down. There's no panic though. I don't care. I'm used to it. The kids are used to it. It take a few minutes but we get back into the game, and I start to feel like the next goal won't be one we're conceding. And it isn't. We equalise. It's the first time all season we've been drawing in a game at a scoreline other than 0-0. My heart's going.

I shouldn't get too excited – we go 2-1 down. Shit. But we get on top again and score. 2-2. We're on top here and it's a bit weird. Do we even dare to win the game? I start to think of this going wrong – we'll end up getting beat again despite being the better team.

I shouldn't worry though. A piledriver from our long-haired midfielder puts us 3-2 up. We're in the lead for the first time in the game. And, the season! Heads are dropping. This time they're not the heads in the red shirts of Ards FC Academy. We don't look back. 3-2 turns to 4-2, 5-2 and it finishes up 6-2.

And now breathe.

I bring the boys in and there's an air of disbelief. Plenty of smiles though and high fiving going on.

Now time to run the gauntlet. This is the walk off the pitch past the waiting parents who are normally all thinking 'that was shit'. It's no gauntlet today though. I swagger off the pitch like I've just tactically masterminded a victory in the final of the Champions League.

I get a few comments from the parents. 'Well done', 'great result Michael', that type of thing. I play it down big time like I knew it would happen. 'Yeah I think that's been coming for a few weeks now, they've been threatening that.'

I get a few 'aye, you're right', 'spot on'.

I'm not convinced, but agree with me if you want to.

My other team are playing at Bangor in just under an hour so I get in my car and head home. It starts to rain as I drive back listening to the Courteeners' *St Jude*. I've been playing this non-stop for the last month or so. It's a 2008 album – I've no idea how it took me seven years to become addicted to it but that sometimes happens. By the time I get back to Bangor, it's throwing it down. Good. I'm from Burnley. I like it better in the rain.

I nip home for a couple of minutes, partly to take a leak, but mainly to have a long-awaited conversation.

'How did they get on?' my wife asks me, shouting from another room.

I answer 'won ... 6-2.'

'What, they won? Really?'

'Yes.'

'6-2?'

'Yes.'

I get to the leisure centre in Bangor and it's now proper pissing it down. It's another AstroTurf pitch – I can't quite describe the surface. It's better than the old hockey surface astros from the 1980s but not as good as the thicker pile 3G pitches. Anyway, despite the heavy rain the pitch is completely fine so there is no need to postpone it. The bigger issue is my wee players; before we start a few of them look like they're freezing. Personally, I think this is great weather for football. Nice slick surface, ripe for slide tackles. Nobody does them anymore. To be fair these astro pitches don't help.

I'm down there early so there's time for the parents to ask me the question about how the other team got on earlier. Normally I dread this question. But not this week. They are surprised to say the least. It ripples around and one tells another, and then the kids learn of the victory. A dad tells his son that it puts added pressure on his team to do the same. Can you imagine? Two wins in one morning? Well yes, I can imagine. You're in the stars today and you owe me big time.

We're playing Abbey Villa for the second time this season. I know that last time they beat us (that's easy to remember) but I can't recall the magnitude of the defeat. The sky might be grey and the rain relentless, as to be expected in February in Northern Ireland. But our start is bright and unexpected. Very quickly, we race into a 3-0 lead. The weather seems to have neutralised the game and most of my players don't seem to have noticed. One of mine is in tears though and walks off the pitch. His dad comes through the gates and says he's taking him home – it's too cold. My coach, Phil, is watching through the fence at the other side, to be near to his car in which his son is sitting (too cold to watch). Abbey Villa pull one back but they're never in the game. We score again. They score. We score.

The rain doesn't give up. My rain jacket is soaking to my skin. My hair sticks flat on my head – the water pressure better than my electric shower at home. Phil gestures to me with a few minutes left – he's heading home.

I look lonely stood on the touchline. I'm feeling anything but. And the pissing rain that soaks me to the bone might as well be the finest champagne. We win 7-4. Two wins and it's not even midday. Its kids' football – it means nothing – but this today means everything. It's a barometer of how far the kids have come – but also, more so, of how far I've come in the last year. It's nothing to do with football, but everything to do with it at the same time. I'm measuring okay. Thank fuck for the football.

Part Two

A YEAR OR SO EARLIER

Tuesday 4 February 2014

My wife works a three-day week and Tuesday is one of her non-working days, so I'm relieved of any domestic duties on a Tuesday. I love a Tuesday. She's only been back at work for two months since maternity leave and I still can't get used to the routine on the days she does work. It means doing stuff that's not for me. It's a right ballache.

I get out of bed at 6.45am. I leave my wife, Catherine, and our two kids, Sam and Oscar, sleeping whilst I attempt to get ready for work without waking them. I go to the bathroom, pick up my razor blade and shaving gel, and look into the mirror above the sink.

'What the fuck?'

I see it straight away. At the top of my neck on the right side of my chin there is … a thing. A bulge. I don't know, it's just weird. I touch it. I touch the opposite side of my neck. It's not the same. This thing, it feels exactly as it looks – it really is there – a bulge. It is rock solid, flesh coloured, no inflammation.

I go back to the bedroom and switch the light on. Catherine is awake – she heard a noise in the bathroom. It must have been me talking out loud. I quickly get a second opinion. We don't know what it is, apart from that it is definitely weird, which falls somewhat short of a medical diagnosis.

Between us, conjuring up all our medical knowledge, and conscious of the fact that medical things and doctors are a pain in the arse, we decide that as this thing has exploded overnight, there's a fair chance it will disappear in a similar fashion. I've maybe slept funny on it and pulled something? Pulled what exactly, well who knows? Pulled a bollock out of my neck. That's what it looks like.

I continue with my normal routine and then drive into Belfast to work. I've just written an article to be included in a magazine and need to get a photograph of myself to go with it. I'm an accountant. The publication is the monthly edition of *Accountancy Ireland*. The article is about corporation tax. Could life get any more interesting, I wonder? I have a few work photos (a work photo being one where I'm wearing a suit and tie – I hate ties, and suits for that matter – and posing sideways on) on my laptop but I look like a bit of a nob in all of them.

I already decided yesterday that I'd get some new pictures and have arranged to meet Chris, the lad from marketing, this morning. I show him the lump and we vary the angles to avoid it. He tells me to get it looked at. I tell him I might do but that it will probably just disappear.

Wednesday 5 February 2014

I'm attending a training session at the Radisson. It's complete bollocks but the coffee is good. I think that kind of sums up every training course I've ever been on in the last few years. I'm touching my neck bollock a fair bit. At one point I'm asked to stand up and talk about a recent audit win. I'm a lucky boy, aren't I? There's about 100 sets of eyes on me. I wonder whether any of them have spotted it. Surely somebody has done, but nobody has mentioned anything to me. I decide that night to sleep on it one more time.

Thursday 6 February 2014

I wait in my car in the car park to make the call. I don't want to do it in an open-plan office.

The receptionists at the doctors treat you as though you've asked them for a blowjob if you ask for an appointment (i.e. they get offended – how dare you ask for that, this is a GP surgery for Christ's sake), so I know I'll have to mention the lump. I do, and get an appointment to see Dr Lavery later that morning. A first-class service, but only if you have a bollock on your neck.

Lavery has a look and feel and says he thinks it's an inflamed salivary gland. He asks me if it's painful to swallow. It tell him it isn't. He asks me if I'm sure. I tell him I am.

He's now unsure as an inflamed salivary gland would normally be accompanied by pain, and I don't have any. We talk about how fast the lump appeared and he tells me he doubts it is anything sinister. Such things would not appear overnight.

He prescribes an antibiotic for the 'inflamed salivary gland' and tells me to come back next Tuesday morning.

'When I see you on Tuesday it will be gone,' he says.

They take some blood and tell me they'll do some blood tests in advance of Tuesday.

Tuesday 11 February 2014

I sit in Dr Lavery's office waiting for him. This is unusual for a doctor's surgery. Perhaps he's popped to the gents.

He finally arrives, takes one look at me, and before he even sits down he says, 'Oh, you'll have to see someone with that.' Well so much for his salivary gland.

He asks me if I have any private medical insurance – I tell him I have it through work. He says that is good and that he'll make some calls for me and call me back later in the day.

He explains that the bloods all look fine, and, whilst not conclusive, would indicate nothing 'sinister'. He doesn't define what he means by this term 'sinister', he doesn't have to, he's talking about cancer and all the other bad shit, and he's pretty much saying I don't have it. Obviously.

He duly calls me later in the day to confirm my private appointment with Mr Rahzan Ullah that Friday, at the Ulster Independent Clinic. Mr? Mr? Don't I need to see a doctor?

Friday 14 February 2014

Mr Ullah is on the phone whilst I wait outside his office. His accent doesn't match his name. He sounds Northern Irish.

He has a good look at it and then says he needs to look in my mouth. That makes sense to me – I've read on the internet that it could be a mouth abscess although I've had a look myself and can't see anything. He then tells me he's going to put a camera up my nose and puts a thin tube inside my nostril. He pushes it up further. And further. It reminds me of something from that episode of *Bottom*, where Adrian Edmondson attempts to remove Rik Mayall's nose hair with a pair of pliers. He tells me that I'm going to 'feel it a bit tight'. What the fuck is he doing?

I ask him, 'How far are you going with that thing?'

'I'm at the top of your nose looking down into your mouth.'

When he said he needed to see my mouth I was expecting him to say 'open wide' and shine a tiny torch in. It's actually painless but the thought of what he's doing makes me shudder.

Anyway, he can't see anything wrong with my mouth either.

He concludes that he thinks it is a bronchial cyst, which has been caused by some kind of irritation.

Fair dos I think. For years I've had a quite aggressive technique for clearing my throat (my uncle once thought there was a wild bear on the loose) so maybe I've irritated it.

Like Lavery, Ullah is confident that it isn't anything more sinister – it came too quickly. Always the way with me.

He briefly explains that surgery will be needed to remove the cyst and draws me a couple of pictures to show me what will get cut off from where. Bit of a ballache, I think, but not the end of the world.

He says we'll need to do an ultrasound and a 'needle test' in order to verify what it is, and that when they put the needle in it will most likely pop and substantially reduce it. Sounds good.

Tuesday 18 February 2014

I'm back at the clinic for the ultrasound and needle test. It's a different doctor tonight.

The ultrasound is all straightforward and we move on to the needle test. The doctor rubs some alcohol on my neck and tells me I'll feel a sharp pinch as the needle goes in.

'Strange,' he says, 'normally you can get a load of fluid out of these, but there's not much coming out, it's so tough.'

I can't help but feel a bit of pride at the toughness of my neck bollock.

He gets the sample and leaves the room. When he returns five minutes later, he tells me, 'It's not a cyst. It's an inflamed lymph node. Sometimes it's nice to be surprised.'

My wife overhears this from the nearby waiting room.

'Nice to be surprised,' she repeats as we're leaving. 'That must be a good thing then?'

'Fuck knows,' I reply, 'you would have thought so but that guy was a bit of a pillock so it's hard to tell.'

Of course, when I get home I google 'inflamed lymph nodes'. I learn that they fall into two categories – harmless and non-harmless. I conclude mine is harmless – my bloods are okay and I'm feeling grand. Plus, something non-harmless (i.e. like, sinister, as the phrase goes) wouldn't just appear overnight.

Friday 21 February 2014

I'm seeing Ullah at 9am. I should be in work for 10am.

'We're going to have to do some talking today,' he says as I sit down. His voice sounds serious. I don't know where this is going now. And I don't really get time to consider the possibilities.

'We've analysed the sample in the lab, and found something called lymphoma.'

I've never heard of lymphoma. Is this good or bad?

He continues: 'Lymphoma is a cancer …'

He finishes the sentence, but I've no idea what he's just said.

Cancer? Did he just say cancer? How can I have cancer?

Words fail me. I simply say 'fuck'.

Several times. He's wittering on at me and I'm just staring blankly at him and saying 'fuck'.

My brain clicks into gear and starts thinking logically.

Hang on a minute mister, surely all we need to do is cut the fucker out. Just like a cyst. It's as you were, minor surgery yeah? Let's draw that picture again but call it something else?

'It will require chemotherapy …'

Now hang on. You told me this was a cyst last week. Your mate said 'nice to be surprised'. Now you're telling me I've got cancer and I need chemo-fucking-therapy.

Of course I don't say any of this. I say little.

'Oh … fuck.'

He hands me a tissue. Only at this point do I realise I'm crying. My head is in my hands.

'Oh fuck.'

He asks if there is anybody with me. Of course there isn't. There was no need. There is nothing wrong with me. Yeah, I knew I was getting results, but not like … not like fucking bad ones. He tells me to phone my wife. I say not yet. I want to know more first.

I know very little about cancer, except that, so they say, if you catch it early enough there's a much better chance of getting rid of it. So I ask him how far advanced it is. It's a good question.

They've no idea. The ultrasound and needle test only looked at my neck, and they need to do a full CT scan to see if it has spread elsewhere.

So I could be fucking riddled? Nice to be surprised.

'Okay, let's do a CT scan then,' I tell him.

'Do you want some time?' he asks me. Yeah, of course. I want to ponder on the fact that I've definitely got cancer but am as yet unsure as to how far gone it is. Do I bollocks want time.

'No. I want to do it now.'

'Okay,' he says, 'we'll get that sorted. Now phone your wife.'

'No,' I tell him. 'Scan first, then I'll call her.'

I'm gambling here a bit. If I call her now not only will she get the worst news of her life, but she'll then be worrying for the next hour or two until we get the results of this CT scan. If I can get this scan done, hopefully it will confirm that it's not spread far and is in its early stages (which it must be, surely). Then I can tell her – that's a much better plan – because then it will be like good news – well not good news, less shitter news. Yes, that makes sense.

They take me back to the waiting room. I'm shattered. It's only 9.30am. How did I get here?

23

A nurse appears and tells me that they'll need to give me something to drink.

'Great,' I say, 'what have you got?'

She laughs. So do I.

I wander over to the water cooler, pour two cups of water, drain one immediately, refill, and walk back to the chair. I drain the other two.

The nurse reappears with 'the drink'. Four cups of it in 45 minutes, spaced evenly. It's needed for the CT scan, she tells me.

She hands me a cup and a huge flask containing a white liquid. It looks like milk. It tastes like shit. It's orange-flavoured white stuff. It's like milk of magnesia. Only worse. And thicker.

There are other people in the waiting room now. I don't know what they're here for. None of them are drinking milk though so it can't be for CT scans. I wonder if they know what I'm doing. I wonder if they think I'm just well into my milk and I've brought this with me. That would be funny. I laugh out loud at the thought.

I cry a bit as well, into my jacket pocket. When it gets too obvious I get up and hide in the bathroom until it stops.

I'm on my third cup of white stuff when another man (in his late 40s/early 50s) is given an equivalent supply of milk. He's sat with his wife. He takes a look and makes some complaint to the nurse, along the lines that he doesn't like it. He sniffs it, sips it, tells the nurse it's okay. I'm fucking glad it's okay mate. I decide that the guy is a nob.

Eventually I'm called into a room to undress. I place my jacket on the hook on the door and put on the surgical gown and robe.

My jacket should be on the back of my office chair on the third floor, not here.

A chap called Tom does the CT scan. I'm still, laid flat on the machine, when he tells me that at 'first blush' there are only inflamed lymph nodes in the neck – i.e. it's localised – and that this is good – an indication of early stage disease. Disease. I've got a disease? He makes it sound like fucking leprosy.

Thank fuck anyway. Some weight falls off the shoulders. He tells me to get dressed and he'll spend another ten or 15 minutes looking at it.

I get dressed and wait. A nurse offers me a drink – tea or coffee this time. It's 11am by now – I tell her I'll take a coffee. A few minutes later a coffee arrives, along with a large scone with jam and butter. A scone? That's exactly what I need. A fucking scone. Oh yes lad, you've got cancer, I tell you what, let's have a scone and see if you're cured.

A chap in the waiting room walks past and points at the tray on the table next to me, and asks where I'd got it from. I tell him that a nurse brought it to me. He sighs. 'Maybe I should come for a CT scan next time.'

I fake smile at his joke. 'You can have the scone mate.'

I see Tom and Ullah go into a room to talk. They're discussing my scan. Ullah comes out and tells me it's my neck only. Now phone your wife.

I go to the bathroom to do this. She answers quickly. I can hear the panic in her voice. This phone call is about two hours later than she was expecting.

I can't say the words, not on the phone. I cry. I tell her to get a taxi to the clinic to speak to the doctor.

I'm back in Ullah's office when Catherine arrives. I'm now relaxed. The tears only come when I think about my family. What if I die? What will that do to my children? Oscar is only one – he will never remember me. Sam is three – he might barely remember me. George (from my

25

first marriage) is seven – he'll remember me, but what kind of dad have I been to him?

Catherine takes a seat. Ullah starts to talk about what is going to happen next (i.e. the treatment). I put my hand up to gesture to him to stop. 'She doesn't know yet,' I say.

He explains it to her. She's upset. I reassure her that all will be fine. I'm pretty composed by now. I'm on an up at the news it appears to be early stages. I listen to little of the conversation.

We sit in the car park. Catherine asks me what I'm going to do about tomorrow.

Tomorrow is Saturday and I've got a long-planned trip back to see the family (Mum, Dad, George) and to go to the Burnley v Forest game. Before 'emigrating' to Northern Ireland in 2007, I'd been a season ticket holder at Turf Moor for almost 20 years, man and boy. It's important to schedule my greatly reduced number of trips home (since the youngest two were born) with a home game.

I should still go, I tell her.

'What about Oscar?'

I'd completely forgotten about that. Our youngest was doing my wife's head in so only a couple of days ago I'd changed my flight booking to add him on – to give her a break for a day or two. I know I can't take him now. There will be far too much to discuss. Plus, I now know that I'm planning to get pissed all weekend. We debate whether or not I should leave it until tomorrow to tell my mum and dad or phone them today.

I dial the number. My mum answers. I don't know how to say it.

'The lump on my neck …'

I start but I can't go on. I break into tears again and pass the phone to Catherine. She finishes my explanation for me.

I compose myself. I take the phone back, and reassure my mum all will be okay.

Her tone is strange, aggressive. She's understandably not taken this too well.

'They will cut it out of you,' she repeatedly near screams down the phone. I know it's not that simple now. This is a blood cancer. It doesn't work like that. It needs chemo. Explaining this is too much for now – it's for another day. Tomorrow. So I agree with her. 'Yes, they'll cut it out.'

Catherine is a mess. I'm feeling okay. I drive us both home.

We stop on the way for cigarettes (Catherine – 20 Regal King Size) and a drink (me – Lucozade Original 500ml). We get home. I eat an apple. I follow it up with a banana.

We pass the time. Sam has been sent home from nursery sick which provides a welcome distraction.

My father-in-law arrives around 5pm with eight cans of Guinness and a bottle of Bushmills. Just what the doctor ordered.

I play darts for hours. I make good progress on the Guinness and Bush. I gather my thoughts. I decide that today is not a bad day. The bad day was at some point in the past when this bastard landed. Today is a good day. Today is the day that we found it and started the fight. It's going to be a great big fucking counter attack and I'm going to kill the fucker.

Part Three

THE LONGEST 37 DAYS EVER

Saturday 22 February 2014
Burnley v Nottingham Forest

I became a Burnley fan sometime in 1986. I was five years old. I was playing out on our front street with our next-door neighbour. He was also called Michael but he was ten. So he was cool. He was wearing a Man United kit. Because of that I was under the illusion that supporting Man United was also cool. The mid-1980s were bleak days for Burnley FC. Attendances dropped to the 3,000 level and we were at the bottom end of the old Division Four. Lots of very young kids supported First Division teams. If it wasn't Man United, it was Liverpool, or Everton even. Definitely not Man City, or Chelsea, or any other southern teams.

Anyway Michael was ten, he was wearing his Adidas Man United kit and he was, in my eyes, super cool.

I was wearing a Burnley kit that my uncle had bought me. It was manufactured by Spall. It didn't even have a Burnley badge on it, such was the state of Burnley's merchandising department at the time.

I liked football. We played on our front street and in the gardens a lot, but I didn't feel any connection to a team. I was only wearing a Burnley kit because it was clothing I owned that my uncle had bought for me.

So as we were out playing, another young lad who I didn't recognise rode down our street on his BMX bike. He had a bag on his shoulder. He was a paper boy.

I'd never seen the lad before, but I could tell he was a couple of years older than Michael, and his name was Nicky.

Immediately, Michael shouted 'Yo, Nicky,' that's how I knew his name.

Michael clearly thought that Nicky was the dog's bollocks.

So, I had thought that Michael was cool. But this lad, he's older, he's on his BMX, and he's delivering newspapers. And he's got a 'y' on the end of his name. This lad is something else. They do not come much cooler than this fine young specimen.

Nicky then starts giving Michael grief for wearing a Man United shirt. I had no idea what was going on. He had a number seven on the back, and it was Man United, surely it was the best thing ever. Then Nicky glances at me, looks back at Michael, and then, nodding towards me, states, 'This lad's got reight idea.'

He turns to me, and then this lad, this ... legend, speaks to me. 'What team do you support, mate?'

I can't get the word out fast enough.

'BURNLEY,' I blurt out.

Nicky smiles and tells me I'm a 'good lad', and then he keeps saying 'this lad's got reight idea' and 'good lad' interchangeably and quite randomly, and throws in the odd high five.

So from that point on I was a Burnley fan, and Man United became my 'First Division team'. You were allowed one in the 1980s when we were in Division Four.

My first Burnley game came in that 1986/87 season. My grandad took me and our Jim. I don't remember the game or who it was against. It might have even been a reserve game.

My next game was against Bolton the following season. And I do remember that one. Not the game, but the end of it. I learnt a new word that day: 'Riot'.

But my third game, again in the 1987/88 season, is what I regard as my first game proper, even though it wasn't. It was February 1988.

I was six by that stage. My dad was going to the game and my Uncle Dave (not my uncle but that's what you called your dad's mates then) was picking him up. For whatever reason, I decided that I had to go. I started off by asking. Moved up a notch to begging. And then resorted to screaming.

I'd shown zero interest before and all of a sudden I went psycho. As my dad got in the car I was still throwing a wobbler on the driveway.

'Paul, I'm phoning your dad,' my mum shouted as he left.

I knew this was a result. Possibly. There was only one reason why my mum was phoning my grandad. I prayed that he would still be at home. It wasn't like she could have called his mobile. If he'd already gone, he'd gone. Luckily for me, he answered. The rest was a formality. There was no way my grandad was capable of saying no to me.

On the way we picked up my grandad's mate Jeff. He owned a newsagent's. That was handy enough. I got back in the car with a quarter of midget gems.

We got through the turnstiles, into the side of the stand, and then turned right up some steps. When I got to the top I was hit by the most glorious sight in my six years of life. Of course I'd been there before, but was too young and just not aware/conscious/hadn't developed a memory. It was a different stand to the one I'd been in before. I could barely remember being there but I knew it was different because it was behind the goal. It felt brand new. The mass of green was enormous, with one of the goals below me and to my left. On my right was the Bob Lord Stand, which I barely noticed. Staring ahead of me was the biggest structure I'd ever laid eyes on. It was a bank of concrete terracing, running down one side of the pitch and continuing around the goal opposite. The long bit down the side (known as the Longside) was covered. It was a wall of noise. A sea of bodies. It looked amazing.

I remember nothing of the game itself. But I was transfixed. I couldn't take my eyes off it. The Burnley Longside. We lost the game 1-0. We were playing Scarborough. But that didn't matter. After that I barely missed a home game for the next 20 years.

I didn't know it at the time but we were in the early part of a renaissance period. The season before the club had nearly been relegated out of the Football League so the only way was up. We finished 1987/88 in a relatively respectable tenth position in Division Four. And we had a trip to Wembley, my first, for the Sherpa Van Trophy Final against Wolves. I still don't know what a Sherpa Van looks like. We lost 2-0 but I don't think any Burnley fan cared. It was a Mickey Mouse trophy. But it was a great day out.

I get the Flybe plane from Belfast City Airport to Manchester and take my seat.

The stewardess is looking at me. She's holding an orange seat belt. It's for Oscar. She looks puzzled. I explain that I'm travelling alone. I start crying. This must look a bit odd. A lone man crying his eyes out, not travelling with the baby he was supposed to have with him. I hope they don't think he's dead. Shit, should I tell her he's not dead, it's just that I've got cancer?

I'm thinking about what to say to them (my mum and dad). The quiet of the plane lets my mind wander. I think about dying. I think about my kids.

I cry a lot on the journey. God only knows what the guy next to me thinks. And so much for my counter attack. As they announce 'ten minutes to landing' I'm in tears again.

I promise myself that once this plane lands I will shed not one more tear for this cancer bastard.

My dad picks me up at the airport. I get in the car. His face looks serious. I realise he's on the phone, well, on the hands-free Bluetooth.

He looks at me and whispers, 'Odds are changing ... just need to get a bet on.'

He finishes his call to Paddy Power. We talk about it. A bit. Awkwardly. Not too much. He's not comfortable.

We talk about George (my seven-year-old from my first marriage). We aren't going to tell him anything.

I've been at their house for half an hour or so when there's a face at the kitchen window. It's Nanna, my mum's mum. She's always here, especially when grandkids are about, just like when we were younger. Different house, different time, different kids – same old Nanna. She's not that old – 79 – but hasn't been in great health for the last year or two – some sort of heart problem – I'm not too sure. She's on all sorts of medication anyway.

I go to answer the door. I wonder if anybody has told her. If they haven't I don't think I should do – I don't want to upset her with her heart problems.

I open the door. She throws her arms around me and says, 'Strong as an ox Michael, strong as an ox.'

Oh shit. She knows.

Later I'm playing football outside with George when my mate Carl phones. He lives in Birmingham but is driving up to the game. He asks me whether I fancy going out in Manchester later. I tell him no but I don't expand. He asks me whether I've had any further thoughts about going self-employed. I tell him I haven't. That's now been put firmly in the long grass. I had been giving it some serious thought towards the end of last year, and at one point was days away from resigning. And then I got a bit of love (i.e. a few quid) out of the blue and it put that decision off. And then it got to Christmas. And then, well, here we are. It's a funny conversation. I've known him 25 years and I've never known this – it's difficult to say anything other than one thing, and I'm not comfortable saying that to him, he's in a great mood, plus he's driving up the M6.

We talk about the game. He's well connected in football circles and tells me a story about two of the younger Burnley players having nights out in London and then flying back first thing in the morning straight back to training. He's clearly not happy about this. I tell him I don't agree and that they have done the right thing.

I have a few pints in the Mucky Duck (White Swan) in Fence and The Talbot in Burnley, near the ground. Taylor's Landlord in both. It tastes like nectar. George is with us. He's at the perfect age for this. Old enough to be able to entertain himself on his DS/my phone, but young enough not to understand the conversations I'm having, openly, about cancer, my cancer. Not so much with my dad, but more his mates. It's helpful, normal. We could easily be talking about getting some guttering fixed.

I've not seen Burnley in the flesh since a 2-0 League Cup defeat to West Ham, and the only league game I've seen this season was a 2-0 win against Yeovil back in August.

Forest are just below us in the league, and on an excellent run of form. They haven't been beaten in ages. If we can win today it will be some marker, some measure of our progress.

I take my seat in the upper tier of the Longside.

The original Longside terracing was knocked down in 1995. Prematurely as far as I was concerned because I'd only just started venturing in there, occasionally swapping my ticket in the Cricket Field End for one in that glorious cauldron of noise. The Longside's last game was against Hull in the 1995/96 season. It felt like a funeral, even for me who had only stood there a handful of times in its last couple of seasons. The regulars who'd called it home for years were distraught. But better to have known it than not. I feel for the kids in there now, sat down and getting bollocked for standing up singing 'we are the Longside, Burnley'. They'd have loved it back then. It really was the finest piece of terracing in the land. I'd been to a lot of grounds before they were completely modified post the Taylor report and didn't see anything a patch on it. Okay, Liverpool had the Kop and United the Stretford End, but it's a bit dull having your popular end as an end. What made the Longside great was that it wasn't an end, it was a long side, with both sets of supporters on it, side by side.

It was a monumental change. Turf Moor is the largest building (and collection of buildings) and also the tallest in Burnley. It sits in the middle of the floor of a valley, surrounded by moorland. Taking that beast down left a gap in the skyline. The house I grew up in was on the outskirts of town, high up on the moors. My bedroom was at the front of the house and looked out over the town. Turf Moor was part of the view, part of the landscape. Just like I saw Pendle Hill every day, I saw the Turf first thing in the morning and last thing at night. But the Longside was the most prominent part of it. My view looked right at it, right at that majestic overhanging roof. I would notice any change, changing the sponsor board that sat on top of it, to replacing roof tiles. When they knocked it down that view changed forever.

By 1995 I was in the third year at secondary school. Turf Moor was only a stone's throw away, separated only by the school playing fields and some low-level housing. The majority of classrooms in the school had a view of the Turf.

I'm not sure whether that was intentional in the design or not. It might have been. There was a football ground at Turf Moor for 80 years before the school was even built, so it's not impossible. For the year or so that they were building the new Longside, and then the Bee Hole End, we had a new distraction. Stare out of the window and watch the build. I think at the time we thought it was pretty shiny and nice and modern. Now I'm not sure. Well I am, I don't like it. The row of executive boxes in the middle breaks the flow, and the roof is too upwards-pointing. I'd love to re-roof it.

My first time on the Longside was April 1988 in the first leg of the semi-final of the Sherpa Van Trophy. We were playing Preston North End, who were at the time in the old Division Three. I looked up to them in awe, having only known Burnley being in the basement division. They were trendy, they even had a plastic pitch, so modern and forward-thinking of them. We were on the Longside; me, my dad and our Jim stood reasonably near the bottom where it was much less congested than at the top, but where you couldn't really see if you were six. It wasn't helped by the fact that the first few steps of the Longside were below pitch level. Looking back, I can't get my head around why they built them like that. The Park End at Everton was worse, it looked like a trench. Or a moat.

There wasn't much to see anyway. It finished 0-0. Coming out of the ground that night though was scary, as in getting off the Longside. There was an exit at the top but most people left via the gates into the Bee Hole End, which obviously had to empty first. You look at modern grounds now and each stand has an exit in every block and within a couple of minutes of the final whistle the stadium is empty and you wouldn't even know there had been a match on. The Longside had one exit of its own and two via the Bee Hole

End, so three exits in total for a bank of terracing that could hold 12,000 people. It was a slow emptier and that night it was busier than normal. We were about ten yards from the gate into the Bee Hole and not moving at all and the crowd was surging from top to bottom of the terrace.

We were near the bottom and the pressure was mounting. I recall saying 'I'm squashed like a sardine,' which, whilst quite embarrassing, is reasonable use of a simile for a six-year-old; we had probably been doing that at school. My dad lifted me on to his shoulders. A lad, he was probably about 25, so much younger than my dad, shouted to the crowd above, 'There's fucking kids down here,' and without feeling the need to ask my dad, grabbed our Jim and lifted him on to his shoulders. Similarly, my dad didn't feel the need to ask whether he was a paedo. Turf Moor changed my view of swearing.

I had formed an early opinion that swearing was very naughty and only bad people swore. But here was a lad, a stranger that we didn't know, trying to look after us whilst at the same time using the word 'fuck'. It didn't make sense at first. But football grounds are for swearing in. They used to be anyway. A place where a man could vent the emotion that he'd been bottling up all week. Fucking shit or fucking brilliant. Just fucking something. A release.

Burnley blow me (and more importantly, Forest) apart in the first half hour and we are 3-0 up at half-time. Complete and utter dominance. I've been going on the Turf since 1987 (though much less since I 'emigrated' in 2007) and never have I seen a performance as accomplished as this. It's been a full 45 minutes (plus injury time) and I haven't thought for one second about this cancer business. It's the perfect tonic.

Forest obviously come out in the second half and do manage to pull one back. It finishes 3-1.

I think about the players on the piss during the week, one of whom had a great game today, putting in a beautiful cross from the right for Sam Vokes to score with his head. I text Carl. 'Not bad for a piss head'. He'll reply, and maybe I can work 'by the way, I have cancer' into the chain that will follow. But that can wait for now. I've beer in my belly and a promotion push on the brain. Fuck you, cancer.

Monday 24 February 2014

I decide that I will need to tell the partner and the HR manager and leave it at that. I don't relish the prospect of telling anybody. I almost feel bad for them. Like, 'here, have that', and see how they react.

By 9.30am that plan is out of the window. Malachy (a colleague who sits nearby) asks 'Hey, what happened Friday? I was worried when you didn't come in.'

Oh fuck, I'll have to say something here. I try to open my mouth but nothing comes out. We're stood up in an open-plan office. I beckon him to follow me to a meeting room.

I find saying it out loud to another person so hard. I don't know whether it's because I find it makes it real, or because of the awkwardness it creates (especially for them). But he's asked me so I will answer him honestly.

My voice nearly gives and I feel as though I'm about to start to cry. But I don't. I tell him what happened on Friday. He's stunned. He thought my appearance in the office this morning was an indication that all was okay, not that I had cancer. I feel great for getting it off my chest. I don't think he does.

Next up, a lad in VAT very casually asks me whether I ever got to the bottom of the thing on my neck. I take him to the same meeting room and tell him. Easy. Not a thought of any tears. I learn that his mum had cancer and that the chemotherapy treatment, whilst it caused complications and side effects, had got rid of the cancer. Success stories. There are plenty of them.

Another colleague tells me about a friend of hers who is undergoing chemotherapy for cancer of the anus and that he is having a terrible time, although his wife has been a rock, but anyway it will be 'pretty grim' for me too. Some people have the ability to say the right thing. Some don't.

My lymph node biopsy is not until 7 March. This feels like ages away. It can't come soon enough. For once. I should stop making that joke.

Tuesday 25 February 2014

My mum phones. She's surprised that I've been to work. She's not the first person to raise this. As I explain, I am not actually ill, I just have a condition which means that I have the potential to be ill if left untreated. But we're going to treat it, and I'm not currently ill. I feel 100 per cent. Why shouldn't I go to work? What else am I going to do? Watch Sky Sports News on loop and once it's looped round too many times start thinking about cancer and death and stuff? No, fuck that for a game of soldiers.

She tells me that she didn't want to worry me … but … Nanna is not well. Why? She's had a problem with her heart. When? Sunday morning. Sunday morning, I was there on Sunday morning. And is she okay now? She's in hospital. She's not conscious. She's not conscious, what do you mean she's not conscious? How long has she not been conscious? Since Sunday afternoon. Oh fuck, she's proper ill.

Thursday 28 February 2014

Today I'm having a proper scan – they tell me it's called a PET scan. I've no idea what PET stands for and don't really care. They key point is, so Mr Ullah tells me, that it's the most accurate scan you can have. It's like the Rolls-Royce of scans. Fuck it, I'll have three of them then. You can't though, they save PET scans for those who are already 'sick'; it's something to do with whatever they inject you with beforehand. He's told me, has Mr Ullah, I can't remember what it is – he might have said uranium? Anyway, they give you some lethal injection instead of force-feeding you milk. Every cloud.

I'm at the Victoria Hospital in Belfast for this one. Again, I don't know why, it's where the appointment letter sent me. I didn't ask. Perhaps they don't do PET scans at the Ulster, who knows? Or maybe this was the first available slot? It definitely feels quick for an NHS appointment. It's like an alternate NHS – like that film, what was it, *Total Recall,* classic – they've a red carpet hiding out the back and they're rolling it out for the big lad.

The format is different from the CT scan. I get 'gowned up' (that's what they call it, not my phrase) so I look like I'm part of a science experiment, and then I'm taken down for my injection.

Then after that, back to an incredibly small room, where I'm meant to lie down for an hour.

There's nothing to drink. In fact, there is nothing to do at all. I don't think I've ever been in a room this small with a bed in it. It's like something from a leisure centre – a changing cubicle – with a bed in it.

Eventually I'm taken for the scan. They strap me down good and tight, much more so than for the CT scan. I've some sort of neck brace on me. They tell me not to move an inch as it will mess up the results. I couldn't if I tried. There is only one 'muscle' they haven't tied down and a hard on is highly unlikely at this stage.

Up and down the tube I go, backwards, forwards, side to side. Intermittently, there's a flash of ultra-bright light amidst the darkness.

What am I doing here? Really? I shouldn't do, but I find this funny. Because you go to work and do stuff. You have a holiday and do stuff, even watching TV is doing stuff. Get your hair cut, have a beer, have a fag. It's all doing stuff.

I've spent most of the morning just lying horizontally on my back, speaking to nobody and seeing and hearing next to nothing. Mainly on my own in a solitary confinement-type box, and partly inside a machine. I'll get back to the office, and they'll ask me where I've been, and I'll tell them, and they'll look at me very seriously, and say, 'was it okay?', 'how did it go?' and 'oh, poor you'.

And I'll be thinking, 'I've literally just been lying down all morning doing fuck all whilst the rest of you pay my wages.' I mean, that's the truth, that's what I've done this morning. Poor me? Really? Sometimes there is nothing crazier than the truth.

Saturday 1 March 2014
Burnley v Derby

I like playing Derby. Mostly because I think we're going to win – we have a good record against them recently and even when at times they've been better than us we seem to get results. And we want one today because, like Forest last week, they're up there at the top and we want to put some distance between us and them.

I've fond memories of Burnley matches at Derby, both the old Baseball Ground and the new Pride Park. Back in 1991/92 when we were still in the old Fourth Division and Derby were in the Second, we'd drawn them in the third round of the FA Cup. A 2-2 draw at the Turf meant a midweek replay at the Baseball Ground. We were 2-0 down when the fog arrived, which led to the game being abandoned with around 20 minutes left to play. As the required time had not been played, the replay needed to be played again, this time on a weekend. Incredibly then, this was a third-round replay being played on fourth-round day. We went to a good number of away games in the early 90s and this one, a Second Division team and not on a school night, was one not to be missed.

We lost the game 2-0 – the result stood this time – but that was irrelevant. What mattered was the noise – the biggest thumping noise I had ever heard and I haven't heard anything like it since. It gives me goosebumps thinking about it.

The away end was a three-tier structure with terracing at the front and two slabs of seating on top of it. We were in the middle tier and pretty central behind the goal. It was cramped, dingy, posts to block your view, wooden seats. With an overhanging roof. It was glorious. They don't make them like this anymore, they really don't. We were one-nil down with about 20 minutes to go when it started – the Burnley fans singing 'Jimmy Mullen's claret-and-blue army' – CLAP – CLAP – CLAP – CLAP. Jimmy Mullen had been assistant manager to Frank Casper when the 1991/92 season started – Casper resigned and, after a successful spell as caretaker, Jimmy got the job. 'Jimmy Mullen's claret-and-blue army' had been the song of choice that season as the Clarets had climbed the table. Normally after five or six renditions it faded out – another song would start or the crowd would get distracted by the game. Not this time, though. It went on, and on. Four thousand Burnley fans packed in – chanting and clapping in perfect rhythm. Everyone was joining in. Every single soul. After a while my arms started to ache so

I banged my wooden seat instead. Others stamped their feet. It was deafening. Our keeper Chris Pearce dropped a clanger to hand Derby a second goal, but the chant didn't break – you couldn't even hear the Derby celebrations. Nobody was stopping – I was ten and getting knackered, but to sit down and draw breath would have been wrong – that would be letting the side down.

The full-time whistle went – we couldn't hear it but the players had left the pitch so it must have done – the noise continued – no Burnley fans moved and it was 15 minutes after the games finished before we started to disperse. We'd been beaten 2-0 and knocked out of the cup, but all 4,000 Burnley fans left the Baseball Ground that day with a smile on their face.

There's a phrase 'it's not about winning, it's about taking part' – I don't like it as it suggests that all a participant needs to do is turn up – they don't – they have to try to win even if they don't. Trying is important. The phrase makes much more sense to me in a football supporting context though rather than as a participant – as in, I don't support Burnley to win, I support Burnley because it makes me part of something fucking beautiful. And win, lose or draw I'm still part of that glorious (yet to many unglamorous) football club where that lack of glamour only serves to extenuate the gloriousness, if you know what I mean. I often feel sorry for supporters of the 'brand' clubs – can they really feel that connection? That closeness, that sense of ownership, like they're in an exclusive club. I doubt that they can. A group of Manchester-based Manchester United fans wouldn't have formed FC United if they did.

That afternoon at Derby was something on a different level though – even as a ten-year-old I actually thought I was part of an army – of Jimmy Mullen's claret-and-blue army and together we could achieve anything. A couple of weeks later the club shop (which in those days was basically a counter) started selling T-shirts commemorating the occasion with a cartoon drawing depicting the away end at the Baseball Ground. Of course, I bought the T-shirt.

In contrast to the Baseball Ground, Derby's new stadium at Pride Park is a modern all-seater bowl. It looks shiny and sharp. But, like most of the modern stadiums, it lacks the character and intensity of its predecessor. It looks a bit like a lot of the others – Boro, Reading, Leicester, etc. These are all new developments on new sites – it's a shame that given a blank sheet of paper they've all come up with the same soulless design. I think it's the bowl bit that annoys me. I prefer the British four separate boxes look rather than something that looks like it's been thrown up in America in readiness for the 1994 World Cup.

I've scored a lot of goals at Pride Park. Unfortunately for me not on the actual pitch but across the way at the indoor soccer dome. I'm going back now to 2000/01-ish when I was at Nottingham Uni – myself and the lads I lived with spent many a Wednesday afternoon over there – it was my first taste of 3G pitches and well worth the short drive over from Nottingham. I fucking loved it, come to think of it. I shouldn't have stopped playing football. It was stupid of me. It was too gradual for me to know it was happening. It wasn't intentional. I've always blamed Nottingham for it. It was probably me.

It was around that time (December 1999) when I saw Burnley win at Derby in the FA Cup. They were Premier League at the time and we were old Division Two (third tier), and obviously Derby were favourites to win. We were on a good run though in our league (which ended up with a promotion) and Derby were doing just average in theirs.

Momentum and morale count for a great deal in football though, two leagues apart doesn't make as much difference if the underdog is in the right mood and the other team isn't. We nicked a 1-0 from an Andy Cooke header in the second half.

I strutted back into Newark Hall with enlarged testicles that night (there were a few Derby fans in there) – it was a giant-killing and it felt great.

Back to today though, it's a bit different – like I find with so many clubs – we're better than we were, and they're not as good as they were. We're improving and they're not. We're both in the Championship now (i.e. so we've moved up and they've gone down) and have been for a few years. And I fully expect to win.

And, of course, if there is any fairness knocking about, I'm owed another win because I've got cancer.

It's never in doubt and we win 2-0 courtesy of goals from David Jones and Dean Marney. Keep improving. Onwards and upwards.

Friday 7 March 2014

Finally the big day arrives and I can't wait. It's been a full two weeks since my diagnosis. You would think I was looking forward to a wedding (or stag do more likely). But no, I'm looking forward to them slitting my throat open and taking some (hopefully lots) of this lump out. Then we can crack on.

It's a day procedure. I've to be there at 11.30am. Hopefully they'll operate early/mid-afternoon and I'll be home that evening. I fast from 7.30am as per the instructions.

By 4pm I'm fed up. Daytime TV is shite. I call for a nurse to see what the situation is. She tells me that it won't be long but there are a couple of small children ahead of me.

This pisses me off on a number of levels.

Why do I need to know that kids are ahead of me? Is it supposed to make me feel bad for asking? Well I don't.

Why do you tell me to be here at 11.30am and then four and a half hours later look at me like I'm crazy when I ask what is happening?

Plus, I'm starving.

I still want to go home tonight so as soon as I wake up after the procedure I sit bolt upright in the bed. I'm in the recovery ward. In fact, I overdo it completely. 'Look at me guys, I'm proper well awake, I am.'

I actually do feel completely fine. No pain in my neck at all. Feels just like a tiny wee scratch.

They let me out at about 9.30pm. When I get home, fish, chips and curry sauce is waiting for me. I inhale it in under five minutes.

Sunday 9 March 2014
Blackburn v Burnley

Of all the football clubs in the world, there is only one that I truly despise. That club is Blackburn Rovers. Otherwise known as Bastard Rovers, or just Bastards for short.

Being only ten miles away, they're our local rivals. And they're fucking Bastards.

I've been brought up with this mindset and everything that has happened since has reinforced those views. The Blackburn badge and blue-and-white halves are symbols of pure evil. I can barely look at them. I played in a corporate five-a-side in Belfast a couple of years ago – one lad on the other team was wearing a Rovers shirt – a legacy of 95 I suspect – glory hunter – purely because he was wearing that I hit him hard first clip and he spent the rest of the game hobbling about. He deserved it.

Of course there was a time when I didn't even know the rivalry existed. My first memory of realising there was something a bit off with this lot was in August 1988. The venue was McDonald's in Burnley town centre. I was there with my dad and brother having a pre-match meal before a pre-season friendly against Blackburn Rovers at Turf Moor. Back then, Burnley were in the old Division Four, and Rovers Division Two. We didn't play each other very often.

So, as we're sat there with our Burnley shirts and scarves on, eating our cheeseburgers, a lad (maybe 17 or 18 years old) and his girlfriend approached us. He had a scarf tied around his waist. It was white with blue-and-red trim, with the words BLACKBURN ROVERS in blue visible across the back. I remember thinking that the way this guy was wearing a scarf was so cool. Then again, I thought those kids on *Home & Away* who wore jeans with their school uniform were cool as well.

The lad asked my dad for directions to the ground. That's all he did. To my surprise, my dad initially refused to tell him, and only after winding the lad up did he let him know to come out of McDonald's, turn left and go straight. I asked my dad why he'd said he wouldn't tell him, and the answer was, 'Because he's a Blackburn fan.' As I would later learn, he was one brave lad to even be in Burnley town centre with that monstrosity around his waist, and my dad's response (by the way, he probably hand-picked us) was by far the best he could have hoped for.

In the next couple of years Jack Walker arrived at Ewood with his cheque book, and after acquiring the services of Kenny Dalglish Rovers were on the up. As Burnley clambered out of the old Division Four, enjoying a revival under Jimmy Mullen, the Bastards were heading for the new Premier League at the start of 1992/93. The gulf between the teams got bigger, the squad and stands at Ewood were being transformed; Burnley were still run on a shoestring in a decaying (but still beautiful) stadium. That only added to the rivalry. And the Bastards didn't deserve it; it wasn't earnt. It was Jack Walker and his money.

I then had my own flirtation with the dark side. I couldn't help it. I was asked and I couldn't say no. The invitation was to the Blackburn Rovers Centre of Excellence. They were a Premier League club, and they'd asked me to attend. I was a mad keen footballer, I couldn't refuse. I told myself it's not about playing for Blackburn, it's about me using Blackburn to make me a better player (not for them, for me). My grandad didn't agree.

I got free tickets to all Blackburn games; I confess that I even went twice during the 1993/94 season, against Liverpool and Swindon. I still had my Burnley season ticket (Burnley and Rovers don't play home games at the same time), but I just went along because it was free. Twenty years later I still feel as though I need to explain / justify my actions. I remember at one of those games a fat lad (a year or two older than me) was sat on the row behind and kept flicking my head and pretending he hadn't. He was that funny. Prick. He was a good footballer, though. He could have been a legend had he not been such a fat bastard. His name was David Dunn but they called him Dunny.

Burnley's revival continued and at the end of 1993/94 we somehow squeezed into the play-offs and won another promotion, into Division One. Rovers, though, had a superb season, finishing third in the Premier League, and going into 1994/95 they were title contenders.

1994/95 was when it all fell apart and cemented forever my hatred of the Bastards. Partway through the season I received a letter from Blackburn Rovers which said that due to FA regulations they had too many players registered and needed to reduce their numbers; they would be monitoring performance over the next few weeks. Not long after that I was asked to play in a match against Blackpool – the one and only time I represented Blackburn Rovers and the only time I have ever worn a blue-and-white halved shirt. It was basically a trial match to assess which players they were keeping and which they weren't. Rovers had a squad of about 25, and they were constantly making changes to give everybody similar game time. I played about 30 minutes at left-back and that was the end of my Blackburn Rovers career. I wasn't too bothered – two nights a week to not enjoy football was not something I was that fond of.

Burnley were out of their depth that year and were relegated straight back down to Division Two. It had looked likely for most of the season.

They won the Premier League, pipping Man United (and nearly losing it – Andy Cole). As Jack Walker and friends cried their tears of joy on the pitch at Anfield, I was in my living room watching Sky crying different tears. Pure agony.

We remained two divisions apart from 1995 until 2000. Miraculously, Burnley were promoted under Stan Ternent into the Championship (second tier), and Rovers, managed by Brian Kidd, were relegated into it only five years after winning the Premier League title. That set up the first league meetings between the sides in years. The problem was Rovers were still on a different level. They beat us 2-0 at the Turf when Kevin Ball got a red for literally going through Dunny (yes, the fat bastard I mentioned earlier) as the anger and frustration spilled over from the fans on to the players. I wasn't the only Burnley fan to take pleasure in that tackle. The away match at Ewood was not fun – we got hammered 5-0. That latter meeting is best remembered for being the longest-ever short journey. At the insistence of the police, all Burnley fans had to travel by official coach. The word 'coach' has been used quite liberally – these must have been a collection of 50 or so of the crappiest buses they could get their hands on. I'm sure retired Burnley & Pendle buses destined for the scrapyard came out of retirement for that one. So, for a 12 noon kick-off, the coaches were leaving Turf Moor at around 9am and we were in the top tier of the Darwen End by 10am. At least they were serving.

Rovers bounced back to the Premier League that season, 2000/01, and we wouldn't meet them again until we drew them in the FA Cup in 2005. A 0-0 draw at the Turf meant a replay at Ewood (which I didn't quite make it to), which we lost 2-1 in extra time.

We had one season in the Premier League in 2009/10 when they beat us twice – 3-2 at Ewood and 1-0 at the Turf.

Luckily, Rovers were relegated again at the end of 2011/12 and we had another two attempts to finally beat them last season. But we didn't – we drew both games – 1-1 at the Turf and 1-1 at Ewood when Dunny popped up with a late equaliser.

Earlier this season we drew with them yet again, 1-1 at the Turf after we'd gone one up and then Jordan Rhodes (their big money signing – cost more than the entire Burnley squad) equalised shortly after. Every player or manager who joins Rovers automatically becomes a Bastard the moment they sign. A lot of them remain a Bastard forevermore, long after they've moved on. Kenny Dalglish and Alan Shearer are two good examples. They'll always be Bastards in the eyes of Burnley fans. 'You'll always be a Bastard,' even though you're a 'Bastard reject'. Unless you later sign for Burnley, that is – if that happens you're redeemed. There's been a few recently – David May, Andy Cole (although when we signed him he'd converted to Andrew Cole) and current midfielder David Jones.

So it's been a long time. Never in my lifetime have we beaten Blackburn (April 1979 is the last Burnley win), so a win today at Ewood would mean everything. To beat them just once, in their own back yard as well. And the thing is, we're above them in the table. We're better than them at the moment. They've spent some money on individuals like Rhodes, but Dyche is building something special at Burnley – we're a proper team. Relentless, we don't say die, and we give maximum effort as a minimum. We can do these fuckers, we really can. It would mean the fucking world. And if this cancer is the price I need to pay to get a victory against them then it might well be worth it. I keep having thoughts like that, like I'm having a private conversation with God – 'Okay God, you got me with the cancer, now hey, lad, how's about, to even it out, you make (yes force it with your magical powers) Burnley win today? Then we're about straight? How about it? Is that what you had in mind anyway? Is this all part of the masterplan? If so, fair dos.'

Luckily, the game is on Sky. Well probably not luck, it's a big derby in the Championship and Burley are second in the table so it was always going to be on – if I'd still been living in Burnley all the TV games would be doing my head in, but for an exile with cancer it's perfect.

During the 1988/89 season we started going to away games more regularly. I used to love an away day watching Burnley; we always brought a good number of fans and quite often outnumbered the home supporters. There was something tribal appealing to me about going to another team's town and bringing so many fans. Like an invasion. Claret and blue everywhere, in places where it shouldn't be naturally. Like we're conquering the town.

An away trip to Darlington sticks in the memory, though. It was one of the first away games I'd been to. The ground itself was a strange one – Feethams. Like Burnley, it had a cricket ground next door. It was a large sprawling site, but pretty decrepit. You had to pay an admission price to get into the ground and then walk for what seemed an age to get to the stadium, and then when you got there, you could watch from the terraces or pay extra to sit in the stand. The away fans were given a full side of the ground, which comprised a small stand on the halfway line flanked by two banks of terracing on either side. I don't remember a great deal about the game. A young couple who had arrived with a baby, literally a really young baby, almost a newborn, argued with the stewards because they wanted to get into the stand without paying anything extra. One Burnley fan, who was in hindsight clearly hammered, climbed all the way to the top of a floodlight pylon. And we found a Burnley pin badge on the terracing after the end of the game. I've no idea what the score was.

The special moment had already happened, much earlier in the day.

We'd got to Darlington quite early and, for whatever reason, I don't know whether it was pre-planned or not, my dad had decided to take us to some sort of train museum first. We'd no real connection to trains, my dad wasn't a trainspotting type, so I've no idea of the rationale, and come to think of it this bit might be dream, but I'm sure trains were involved. But anyway, the special moment wasn't train related.

It was after the train museum. We were somewhere in Darlington, but away from the ground. Maybe near the trains? It was a park, or a square, some place with grass and park benches but still built up, perhaps in the town centre.

We were sat on a park bench. There were roads that went around the square.

My dad spotted it first because he recognised Jones Executive as a Burnley brand. Burnley's brand of executive buses. It was the Burnley team coach stopped at the traffic lights right next to the park/grass square where we were sat. In a flash I was off on my feet sprinting to the coach, my Burnley shirt complemented by the scarf I was waving above my head.

The first Burnley player on the coach to see me was Steve Gardner. He smiled right at me, or more like grinned, then pointed at me, beckoning other players to have a look, and in a second there were four or five players with Steven Gardner in the centre, waving at me. The lights turned green and they were off. My brother and dad caught up with me. They missed out.

Steven Gardner smiled at me, pointed at me, waved at me. I was over the moon.

Steve Gardner had signed for Burnley in 1987 aged 19, after being released by Manchester United without breaking into the first team. He made over 100 appearances in three years at Turf Moor, before being released in 1990. He played 14 times for Bradford and just once for Bury before quitting professional football in 1992 aged just 24.

Football creates heroes. They come in all guises and shapes and sizes. Steve Gardner is one of mine.

We start okay, it's a bit tight and tense, but go a goal down in the middle of the first half. Rhodes again. We just keep going as we are – there's no panic, no rush. There's a discipline about this Burnley team that Dyche has instilled – we don't lose our heads. As half-time nears I get into that thought process of 'please just keep it to one until half-time, don't let another in now and give ourselves a harder task'.

We never look like we're going to and it remains 1-0 to the Bastards at half-time. Sean's got this in hand – he will be measured – he won't get carried away – there's not a lot we're doing wrong really. I feel strangely confident. We've not beaten them for 35 years and we're 1-0 down away from home. But I think we'll win.

We come out for the second half searching for an equaliser – time ticks by but I'm certain we're going to score, and once we get one we'll have all that momentum, shooting towards the 5,000 Burnley fans in the Darwen End, then we'll surely get another. I just know it. This is what Dyche has done to us this season – we're not stressing, just an absolute belief that we can do it and not accept defeat.

With just under 20 minutes left, we get the breakthrough as Jason Shackell heads in from a corner for 1-1. I'm now dancing around my living room and the kids wonder what the hell I'm doing. Even though I'm watching on TV, I don't sit down – I watch standing up, about three yards from the screen. It's got to be done. Get well and truly worked up. Only for Burnley matches. I sit down for games in which I'm a neutral (and when England are playing I normally do something else like change the batteries in my torch and have it on just as a bit of background noise).

Six minutes later we're in dreamland as Danny Ings taps in to put us 2-1 up. We're winning. At Ewood. Against the Bastards. Now then Burnley, don't fucking blow it now. Hang on. I need not worry. We stand resolute and win 2-1.

Fuck me. We've done it. We've beaten the Bastards. God, you work in mysterious ways and the cancer wasn't ideal, but thank you for this glorious moment. Despite Walker's millions and acquiring the Premier League title, we're above you, and we've beaten you. Because we're better. Because we're Burnley. So fuck you Jack Walker and Kenny Bastard. And fuck you Dunny.

And as for cancer, well then my friend, since I was diagnosed we've won three games on the spin so you can fuck off too. Burnley 3 Cancer 0.

Wednesday 12 March 2014
Birmingham City v Burnley

Tonight it's an away game against Birmingham City. It's winnable, they all are at the moment. But any away game in the Championship where anyone can beat anyone is difficult. And Birmingham are one of the bigger clubs in the league.

As usual I'm following the games watching Sky Sports News. It's better midweek as there are rarely Premier League games on so the Championship gets much more attention.

I watch the game standing up with a football at my feet. I'm not even watching the game; I'm watching a few middle-aged blokes talking about games that they're watching on monitors, and every so often they talk about our game.

After 30 minutes, we're ahead through a Dean Marney goal – 1-0 Burnley and I'm hoping we don't hear from St Andrew's again all night. We don't for a while, and then it goes a bit crazy. First, Macheda (on loan from Man United) equalises in the 64th minute. Then, just three minutes later, Michael Duff puts Burnley back in the lead, 2-1, with a rare goal for him. Then two minutes after that Huws (on loan from somewhere else) equalises again for Birmingham with a wonder strike. I'm raging. Time ticks on. It looks like we're settling for a point. Until, that is, our own Welsh legend Sam Vokes pops up in the 86th minute to put us back in front with a trademark header. I'm fucking loving Sam Vokes at the moment. More than Danny Ings. Vokesy has had a strange career, only young but shipped and loaned about and never quite done it. Never really put down roots anywhere, hasn't had the chance, and started this season on the bench, only playing since we sold Charlie Austin to QPR to pay the bills. And he's doing great, scoring a good few and making some, and holding the ball up well. Proper old-fashioned English centre-forward. Okay British, Welsh, whatever.

Macheda you Italian pillock. Just when I think we have the three points in the bag (by the way what type of bag? A satchel) we go back to St Andrew's. They boys in the studio are saying it's handball. Let's wait for the replay before getting too cross. It's a blatant handball. The game finishes 3-3. None of the Brum scorers play for the club and one goal shouldn't have stood. I'm gutted. We've been robbed.

Okay, I've got cancer. I should put this in perspective. Okay, I have done. It really matters.

Thursday 13 March 2014

The biopsy (or autopsy as one of my work colleagues keeps saying – don't write me off just yet) really was easy.

The wound is small and painless. The lump is still big, though; he must have only taken a wee bit out.

The clinic told me to visit the GP surgery on Thursday to get the stitches taken out. I say stitches, they are more like staples. And so I have arranged to have that done today. Naturally, that wasn't easy. The receptionist at the GP surgery acted as though I had asked her to give me a kidney. Apparently, the clinic should be removing the staples and not the surgery. Does it actually matter? No.

The nurse is pleasant enough. She asks if I have had the results of the biopsy yet and I tell her no, but I already know the headline, just not the subtype.

She's shocked. I'm not sure whether at the diagnosis or my nonchalance about it. Shock is the usual reaction.

The wound is infected. She thinks the staples have been left in a day or two too long. She prescribes an antibiotic.

Everything is normal. I still go to work. I have a few appointments to do but other than that, life goes on. I still feel fine. And these things that I have to do are not too bad; in fact, it's a bit of variety – new people and new experiences. I'm still allowed to laugh, and, as ever, there is humour in a lot of places in this world, you just sometimes have to work a bit harder to find it.

I've never had so many medical appointments, seen so many waiting rooms, or overheard so much aimless chit chat.

As I'm waiting to see the nurse there are a couple of old dears. They'd be late 70s, similar to Nanna. One has a heart condition, the other a bad back. They're talking about modern food versus food when they were lasses and it is hilarious. Out of nowhere one of them emphatically declares 'I love champ' and I almost laugh out loud. I'm not part of the conversation until one of them turns to me and asks, 'Do you eat pizzas? I bet you do, don't you.' There's an accusatory tone to her question. And she's asking it with a hint of humour. Like she's laughing at me for suspicion of modern eating habits such as eating pizza.

This is different; it's funny in a new way. I'd never get this sat in the office.

I do eat pizza, sometimes. It's okay. My preferred takeaway food is Indian because it gives me an excuse to drink copious amounts of Cobra or Kingfisher in those big 660ml bottles. Nice and cold. Hang on, whatever happened to Lal? Lal Toofan? Where did it go?

Friday 14 March 2014

I take a call from Mr Ullah. He's got all the test results now. The biopsy and the PET scan. It's Diffuse Large B Cell. God knows what that actually means. The relevant fact though is that it's the most common type of non-Hodgkin lymphoma, and because of that it has the most established treatment programme. This is good news.

Diffuse Large B Cell, get in! I celebrate a relative victory.

When he first said non-Hodgkin lymphoma the other week I didn't really get it. The 'Non' bit was confusing. He said NON-Hodgkin lymphoma, and I was thinking, 'If this isn't Hodgkin lymphoma, then what exactly is it?'

I then gathered that what he meant was that it was definitely lymphoma, but just not of the Hodgkin variety. So, what, are all lymphomas either Hodgkin or non-Hodgkin?

Who the fuck was Hodgkin? Fair dos, he discovered something and they named it after him, I get that bit. But then, every other lymphoma, ones he had no clue about, he gets a mention of his name in them as well? That's just greedy!

What about your man who discovered Diffuse Large B Cell (his Mrs must have suffered)? He must be raging! What's his name? I bet he hates Hodgkin. It's all about him, isn't it?

Saturday 15 March 2014
Burnley v Leeds

Leeds aren't doing great but it's the same issue as a load of these big teams. They're big. The Championship is full of big teams doing worse than they ought to. It makes them a bit more scary even if they're currently crap.

I've no time for Leeds. They're ugly. Dirty Yorkshire Bastards. And that's probably a compliment. Obviously for the early part of my football life we didn't play them, we were usually at least two divisions apart, so my dislike of them isn't Burnley-related. It's just the mental picture in my head. My first awareness of them was the 1988 play-offs when they made the papers for burning down beach huts in Bournemouth. It feels as harsh writing that now as it sounded then. Beach huts, in Bournemouth. It's like fighting with a smiling, helpless puppy and then claiming a victory. They then did very well for a period of time and won the old Division One in 1992 (the same year we won the old Division Four) and at that stage they were inoffensive. Subsequently, though, over a period of years, I realised that their star striker was an alleged wife-beater, their midfield maestro a whiny Scot with a chip on his shoulder, and the manager a very average one who sold Eric Cantona for a pittance. The media have played their part as well. It's funny, that; Leeds get a lot of grief, and even the great Leeds team of the 70s have gone down in history as a team of thugs. That image of Johnny Giles throwing punches at Wembley during the Charity Shield doesn't help the Leeds branding cause. The fact that he was throwing them at a player of the class of Kevin Keegan only makes it worse. Billy Bremner trading punches with Franny Lee is another. And there's another factor. One that influences my dislike of them even more than some of their dickhead fans buying tickets in the Jimmy Mc Lower in the mid-2000s. Clough.

Brian Clough is probably the most fascinating manager the world has ever seen. Brilliant, slightly crazy, but genuine and honest. I read his autobiography when I was about 12 and fell in love with the man. The later *Damned United* book and film dramatise his short spell at Leeds. It didn't go well. There is plenty of that book where gaps are filled in with fiction, but the best bits are the real stuff – the TV interview with Don Revie (watch it on YouTube) is legendary. The upshot, Leeds got rid of Clough. He went to Nottingham Forest and became, in relative terms, the most successful British manager ever (a league title and two European Cups). Whether he meant to or not, Clough caused permanent damage to Leeds. And we have to love Clough. Especially at the moment. Dyche was a youth player at Forest and got his first professional contract there, under Brian Clough. There's a bit of Clough in Dyche.

Leeds' big-money signing Ross McCormack gives the away team the lead just before the half-hour mark, but a few minutes later an own goal makes it 1-1 at half-time. Midway through the second half, Scott Arfield puts Burnley ahead for the first time and, unlike Wednesday night, we don't let the lead slip.

Burnley win 2-1. Back to winning ways.

I also get back on track with betting. Since I've been diagnosed I've stopped my weekly football betting. I guess for a few weeks I just didn't see the point. As in, if I win, then so what? What good is a few quid going to do me? It's no good to me if I'm dead, and I'm not going to win anyway so why waste the money?

I'm thankfully over that phase. I put a few accumulators on and lost the lot. It's great. Not losing money, but wanting to win. Welcome back. It's years since I won anything decent though, 2005 in fact.

Steve Cotterill had replaced Stan Ternent in the summer of 2004. Tipped as one for the future, he hadn't exactly lived up to that in his first few months at Turf Moor. He had brought stability at least, though, we weren't as erratic as we'd been under latter Stan, and we never looked like we'd get hammered.

We'd drawn Liverpool at home in the third round of the FA Cup, who themselves had a new manager that season, a certain Rafa Benitez. The game was originally scheduled for a Friday night but was called off due to the weather and subsequent state of the pitch. By that stage, though, the teams had already been announced. I couldn't understand what Benitez was doing – he'd named a team of kids who had barely played any first-team games between them. I couldn't tell whether it was arrogance or whether he was just another foreigner who had no clue about English football beneath the top flight, and was he assuming it was like the second tier in countries like Italy and Spain? One thing you can say is that it's not Rafa.

Even though I was constantly skint at the time and my salary as a trainee accountant barely covered my car, petrol and mortgage (never mind my mounting credit cards and non-existent wedding savings), I knew what I had to do by the time the rearranged game came around. Again, it was a night game. It was January, nice and cold and pitch black. I found some mugs on Betfair who were laying at 7/1 for Burnley to win. I bet £50 that I didn't have to spare on it.

Rafa didn't let me down. He picked largely the same team of kids as he had planned to the previous week. I don't remember ever being so confident of beating a team from a division above. Burnley dominated the game but, as it had been under Cotterill so far, we didn't create many chances or take many risks. It needed a comedy own goal from Djimi Traore in front of my new home in the Jimmy Mc Lower to put us into the lead following a Richard Chaplow cross. We saw the game out to win 1-0. And I'd made £350 profit thanks to Rafa. I wonder how fast I'd be able to waste that. You never know, maybe he was saving the big guns for the Champions League.

Tuesday 18 March 2014

Today is my first meeting with the haematology team at the Ulster Hospital. I've been to this hospital before. Sam and Oscar were both born in the maternity unit, Oscar just 14 months ago. It feels like decades.

I haven't seen the rest of the hospital. I quickly realise that, despite the modern foyer, it is a complete tip. I should add that the maternity unit is new – it was clouding my expectation. The rest of it is just dreadful. It feels a bit like my old school; that you're outside even when you're inside. But not in a Walt Disney World type of way. This is more like, surely there are no interior spaces as bad as this. Did it really need walling and roofing? You kind of feel that you might get mugged as you walk around a corner, as though it's some sort of underground city of the future.

We are near the restaurant. The smell of overcooking vegetables, BO, sweating onions and old peoples' piss hits my stomach. We stop our exploring and turn around.

My appointment is for 9am but the letter I got tells me to report to Reception Two a minimum of 30 minutes before the appointment time. I am surprised to find that Reception Two is closed at 8.30am, and even more surprised to learn it never opens at 8.30am. It opens at 9am. Every single day. Well, what a crafty letter that was.

We wait. There's not many in the waiting room, just a couple of old couples. I'm guessing between the four of them the combined age is circa 340 years.

Just before 9am a young girl opens up Reception Two. I'm eager to go over but no, I'm a professional. I'll give her a few minutes to get settled, take her coat off, log on to her PC or whatever she needs to do.

One of the old timers though is straight up talking to her, and before I know it she's being led somewhere by the nurse. Then the other geriatric gets up and the same thing happens.

What do I do? The poor girl hasn't even sat down yet. I panic. My wife panics. These old timers are the real professionals. They've been there and bought the T-shirt.

Then from out of nowhere there's a stampede of them. Zimmer frames and grey, bald and limping, all heading towards Reception Two. Where did they all come from? I get up to join the scrum.

I get checked in and sit back down again. A few minutes later a nurse calls me. She takes my weight and height, and leads me into a small room. There are three chairs on one side, two of them are occupied, the third I sit down into. They're doing some blood tests. Clearly, if I have blood cancer, I'm expecting my blood will fail the test. It doesn't work like that though – they're testing for lots of different things/properties. I'm going to have to get used to this. There will be some needles. I've no problem with them. I've never been squeamish and I can look at my own blood, no issue. She gets the needles in my arm and starts to draw blood out. I watch as each tube is filled rapidly. I can't even feel anything yet this liquid is pouring out of me. She's filled about five tubes and then pauses, and turns to me.

'This last one,' she looks at me awkwardly, 'is to test for HIV … is that okay?'

I'm taken aback. Why is she asking me this? Is this what they normally do? She hasn't explained what the other samples were being tested for so why is she mentioning this one?

'That's fine,' I say, wondering what that is about.

I'm back in the waiting room waiting. There is a lot of this. Lots of time investment. Not much action. I'm now waiting to see Dr Ong. So I'm looking for a doctor. I don't even know if Dr Ong is male or female, but I'm looking for a doctor type.

The consulting rooms run down two sides of a large square waiting room in the centre, so the doc could be anywhere. A Middle Eastern bloke is scratching his head by one of the rooms. Of course, that's me. He's wondering how to pronounce my name.

He sits me down in the room, my wife is with me. His name is Dr … I don't quite catch it, but he's not Dr Ong. He has a nurse with him, Joanne.

He takes a few details but he's distracted. He's transfixed by the lump on my neck. My tumour. 'It's very large,' he says. I know that Sherlock, I'm living with the monster. 'It's got a lot bigger,' he goes on. He's reading his notes and at some point somebody previously has measured it.

'I'm not sure it has,' I tell him.

He looks back at the papers. He takes a tape and measures it – 13cm long. He looks back at his notes and tells me it says 7/8cm.

'I don't know who measured it at 8cm, but doing it the way you've just done it, it's never been 8cm.'

In my mind, and my wife agrees, the tumour is about the same size as it was when it landed.

In reality it landed massive, got a bit smaller once the biopsy took a chunk out of it and then grew again. But it's never been 8cm.

'I think you'll need to have another PET scan.'

Oh, for fuck's sake. This is bad on two counts. First, it's just another delay, it will take time. Second, it means they think based on the size (and apparent growth) of this tumour, that the cancer has spread.

The nurse gets involved now. 'When did you have your PET scan, love?'

'A couple of weeks ago, is that where the measurement you're getting is from? You're measuring different things then, if you put a tape measure against this it has always been 12/13cm.'

The Middle Eastern guy now seems happier.

'Okay fine, if you only had a PET scan two weeks ago, it can't have grown so much since then.'

He finishes his admin and observations and then all four of us go into a room next door. Finally, I meet Dr Ong and realise it's a she. Middle Eastern guy (who, I learn, has a name – Dr Alshoufi) leaves, so we're back down to four. It then gets a bit strange. I'm probably slightly unusual in that I have been mixing and matching NHS and private medical care. I had the big picture diagnosis weeks ago. Mr Ullah has since told me the score re the biopsy and PET scan. The way this is all set up – Dr Ong at one side of the desk, me, Catherine and Joanne on the other side – she's with us – gets me thinking. There will be a good number of people who come to meetings like this and get the shock of their lives. I've already been diagnosed. It's been gradual over the last few weeks but I know the full story. She's looking at me like she's about to deliver something life-changing. I'm going to disappoint her here.

She tells me they have looked at the PET scan and biopsy results and I have non-Hodgkin lymphoma. I tell her I already know. She explains that they have a sub-type for me. It's Diffuse Large B Cell. I tell her I already know.

She looks at us and says, 'Are you okay? I have to say, you two both look very calm.'

Surely she knows that I know all this.

'Well we already know all this, Mr Ullah has told me.'

She should have seen me crying in the toilets at the clinic the other week. I've not cried like that for over 20 years. Not since that England v Scotland match.

It was February 1992 and England were playing an under-16s schoolboy match against Scotland at Turf Moor. Before it, there was going to be a 15-minutes each way under-11s game, East Burnley against West Burnley. I'd no idea what this East and West was about, but basically it meant that they were splitting the primary schools in Burnley into two groups and picking a team from each. We, it seemed, were in the West. I was so excited at the thought of playing on the Turf. And I knew for certain that I had a great chance of making the team.

For some reason our school team manager, Mr Foster (known as Fozzy), only sent three of us for the trials: myself, Woody and Stanny. He could have sent more but maybe some of the others wouldn't have got in the team. I was convinced that all three of us were certs after the trial matches.

He broke the news to us together. As soon as he said, 'Michael, I'm sorry,' I burst into tears and ran off to the bathroom. It was my first disappointment in my football life, in my life in fact. Woody and Stanny, who had made the team, tried to comfort me, but I was inconsolable.

Fozzy drew the short straw here and it wasn't even his decision.

'Michael, you will play on the Turf one day ... you'll walk into that team at St Theodore's, and you'll play in the Keighley Cup Final.'

The Keighley Cup Final was a secondary school competition, and every year the final was played on the Turf. I knew all that. I also knew it was for fourth-years. Four years away!

I still wanted to go to watch the match. Despite being massively jealous, I wanted to watch my friends. I almost cried looking at the teamsheet in the programme knowing my name should have been there. I looked at the bench and regretted being a right-back because benches (of two or three) were usually made up of forwards or midfielders.

West got beat by East. I couldn't have cared less.

England played Scotland and won. During the game a ball got stuck behind the advertising board on the Longside roof. A few days later, two Burnley FC apprentices were sweeping the Longside as part of normal apprentice duties in those days. They decided to climb up on the roof to retrieve the ball. One of them, Ben Lee, fell through a roof tile and dropped 60 feet on to the Longside terracing. He died. Football. Life. Death. Fuck.

'And do you have any questions about the diagnosis?' she asks.

'No.'

'No?' she says.

What sort of questions is she looking for? Of course, in the last few weeks the term has been googled to death. Not by me. But the rest of the world has been at it and they tell me what they've found. Statistics, chances, survival, death. All that good stuff. I'm not fussed on yet another viewpoint. I am what I am. I'm my own statistic and nobody else's.

'I'd like to know about the treatment.'

Bloody hell. This is all that matters. I've no interest in what this thing is. That's completely academic to me. All I care about is what we're going to do about it.

'Okay, yes, we had the multidisciplinary-team meeting,' she starts.

Ullah had told me about this. It's some sort of round-table discussion where various doctors discuss treatment programmes for patients. For my cancer I have picked up that it doesn't just need a cancer doctor (an oncologist) but also a haematology specialist. I can't picture what this meeting looks like. Are they around a boardroom table like we are at work? Drinking coffee and talking crap. Or is it by conference call? I bet it's all a bit serious. I prefer my job to this. I can't work out where they find room for banter. Can you have cancer banter?

'And you have a choice …'

A choice? No, no, no, just tell me what the job is. Love, I don't want to choose. Just keep me alive as you doctors think you should.

'The chemotherapy you will have is R-CHOP.'

She tells me the names of each drug in the cocktail so fast I can't recall what they are. But I don't really care.

'You could have three cycles of R-CHOP, and probably some radiotherapy treatment.

'Or you could have six cycles of R-CHOP and probably not any radiotherapy.'

Nice one. I just love making decisions like this. I'm struggling.

'Okay. What's better?' I ask her. Is that a daft question?

'It depends, there are pros and cons of each … there is only a finite amount of chemotherapy that someone can take in a lifetime, that's the downside of having six cycles.

'If you have three cycles and radiotherapy, it should work, but probably a marginally smaller chance of getting rid of it completely. But you have some chemos saved. But the radiotherapy has a slim chance of causing secondary cancers.'

'And you want me to decide this?'

Bugger me. Just tell me the answer, woman.

'Well, there is no right or wrong answer … but at your age … you don't want just to manage it … you want to try to eradicate it … so the six.'

'Okay then, the six.'

'But then there are risks with that in that the chemo weakens the heart and the body can only …'

Oh, come on.

'We'll come back to you on it.'

'Okay, and what exactly is a cycle?'

'It's a three-week cycle. On day one, which will be a Monday, you'll come to the McDermott Unit for chemotherapy. The rest of the cycle you're at home.'

'So, I'm not here overnight?'

'No, it will take most of the day, especially the first time, but you'll be home in the afternoon.'

I'm staggered by this. Is that it? I thought this was going to completely occupy my life. Is she really telling me it's one day out of every 21?? I can do that.

'There are tablets to take at home, for weeks one and two, week three is recovery, and then the next cycle starts.'

Tablets? Just tablets? I can do this. I thought they'd chain me to a bed for months, whilst using needles to insert things in my head.

So, it's a few injections and a few tablets. This whole thing is kind of growing on me. I'd rather not be here but it all seems a bit more straightforward than I was expecting. At every new corner, it's like, yeah okay that's grand, and I don't feel too concerned. Bring on the chemo!

Dr Ong is looking at the diary. '31 March, that's a Monday, so you'll come to the McDermott Unit first thing.'

'That's only ten days away so you need to have a bone marrow biopsy …'

'What's that for?'

'To check if the cancer has spread there. We don't think it has but we need to check. And you'll need a heart scan echo to check your heart … and … is your family complete?'

Is my family complete?

It takes me a few seconds to work out what she means. I am presuming the answer is yes but me and the missus haven't really talked about it. Yes. No. Who knows? Definitely not me, that's for sure.

'The reason I ask is that the chemotherapy you will have will probably make you infertile ... so if you are undecided whether your family is complete you might want to consider sperm banking.'

I'm not sure I knew about this bit. Infertile? I can't tell if I'm bothered. Do we want more kids? I don't know. And I don't know what the right answer is. The ones we have are difficult enough.

'And you probably don't have time to decide so you might as well do it, just in case.'

I'm going to be a busy man at this rate.

Dr Ong looks at the stuff Dr Alshoufi was writing down.

You know, I bet she's never even heard of Dyche. And she thinks she knows all about beating cancer. She can't know it all if she doesn't know about Sean.

'And Mr Heinicke, how much alcohol do you drink?'

Well, whatever I told Dr Alshoufi is written down right in front of her. Why is she asking?

'Yes, normally about, typically, on average, circa, approximately 28 units, give or take.'

This is my standard answer. From memory this is the maximum recommended intake for a male. I'm lying through my teeth.

'And what do you drink?'

'Mainly beer.' I'll leave out the whiskey for now. If I include it the next bit just gets daft.

'So that's about 14 pints of beer per week.'

Lol, it sounds like nothing when they translate it to pints. I feel my wife's eyes on me. I can't look at her. She knows this is all complete lies.

'Yeah probably, maybe 15, on average, you know.'

'Okay. It's too much. You need to cut down.'

'Yes, I will.'

The problem with being diagnosed with cancer is that I want to drink more, not less. It's all a bit, like, stressful.

'So, hang on … has drinking contributed to this, do you think?'

'No,' she replies. Good, I'll crack on then.

'But alcohol isn't good for your immunity, and the chemo will weaken your immunity anyway. You need to cut down.'

'Yes, I will, sure … but not completely though?'

'Halve it, can you do that?'

Well this is an interesting question, is she telling me to halve what I've told her, or to halve what I actually drink? The latter will be infinitely easier than the former.

'Yep.'

The next 'phase' of this check-in procedure involves me being led into another room off the side. It's like three rooms in a room with interconnecting doors. She asks that my wife waits where she is.

Dr Ong and Joanne accompany me to the examination room and ask me to lie on the bed, take my shirt off and loosen my jeans. Blimey, what are they going to do to me? It reminds me of my old school, St Ted's. Before I even started there were rumours that when you got to the end of the second year the school nurse did a 'test' to check that you could ejaculate. Like 120 lads. But it was just part of her job. Nothing sexual about it from her point of view. But for about two years I was shitting myself.

Over time, not so much due to physical growth but more not being so gullible, I gradually became less concerned about this. For clarification, it was, like many stories that flew around St Ted's, complete fucking garbage.

'Now, Mr Heinicke ... you're a young guy,' she's looking at me and I have no idea where she is heading with this. 'So, if there is anything you want to tell us then you can ... in relation to ... your sexual activity.'

Hold on, what are they trying to say?

'Because, you can tell us ... and it's important because ... there are very few risk factors for non-Hodgkin lymphoma ... but HIV is one of them.'

Oh right, that's no bother, just a bit of HIV then. The fun just never stops. Next they're going to touch me. She feels around my chest, pressing hard in all the areas where lymph nodes are likely to be inflamed. Unfortunately, there are lymph nodes in your groin. She slides her cold hand underneath the waist band of my boxer shorts and starts to feel around. She only gets as far as the top of my pubic hair and then she's finished. Well done. I applaud myself for avoiding getting hard.

Even then we're not quite finished. Joanne leads me and my wife out the room (or the trio of rooms I should say – very strange design) and into another room. It's all sofas and coffee tables. Oh blimey, this is like one of those 'bad news' rooms you see on the tele, they have them in hospitals. And I'm in the bad news room with the nurse and my wife and we're playing the part of the victim. But it's surreal. Because it's not bad news. Not today. I haven't just been diagnosed.

Joanne makes comments again about how calm we both are. But Joanne, we already know. We're over this. It's yesterday's news, so the normal drill doesn't apply.

Joanne gives me a 'pack'. There is all sorts of stuff in it, booklets, leaflets, and a thermometer. For free. It's like freshers' week at uni when you get all sorts of freebies. Except there are no condoms or alcopops. To then top it all, she gives me a free car parking pass to the hospital. Result. Relatively, that is.

It's a long appointment, but I feel satisfied. Like I've achieved. Even though I've done nothing but turn up. I have a start date, Monday 31 March – ten days to go. I can't wait. Bring on the chemo. Get it into me. Every last drop of it. Before then I need to have a heart scan, a bone marrow biopsy, go to an 'open day', and decide if we want more kids. Wow. It's all happening now. It's like preparing to go on holiday. Well, not quite but I'm making final preparations for an event though.

This is good, this is progress.

Wednesday 19 March 2014

This is just pure weird. They've not called it an open day, that's my word for it, but it's a talk and a tour of the cancer centre for new chemo patients in advance of starting treatment. Albeit it's probably not a case of 'I don't fancy this one so I'll have a look somewhere else'. More of managing expectations.

The talk takes place in a meeting room in the breast cancer centre.

I shouldn't but I feel like a bit of a pervert being in there. There are six new patients, each with a guest. I keep thinking of that film *Willy Wonka and the Chocolate Factory*. Catherine is with me. We're the youngest people in the room by some distance.

The only other male is Bob. He's old, and he must be 80 if not older. His daughter is with him.

I've personally done very little googling of chemotherapy so this is a worthwhile lesson for me. The six patients in the room all have different cancers. Everybody is having a different form of treatment. All chemotherapy. But different types of chemotherapy. Some are having radiotherapy (which isn't listening to Radio 2) as well. I'm not yet but I might be if required.

Not everybody's hair will fall out. Years ago I used to think that cancer made people's hair fall out. You know, cancer people. Those unfortunate ones. But I knew even before today it's not the cancer, it's the chemo. But now apparently it might not even be the chemo. It depends on the strength of the chemo cocktail you're having. I didn't know that.

The nurse goes around the room and says whose hair will fall out. I'm marked as being one that will lose my hair. Luckily I don't really give a fuck. I've shaved my head in the past many times out of choice so doing it not out of choice isn't much different.

I do have a question though. Feels a bit keen to ask doesn't it, but I'm curious around the timing.

'So, how does this work?' I say. 'How does it fall out? Like straight away, or the next day? Or what?'

'Probably ten days to two weeks after your first treatment it will start to fall out.'

'Nah,' I'm thinking. Not me. That's maybe the normal state which applies to everybody else, but not me. Not that I'm bothered about my hair. But mine won't fall out. I'm too young. I'm too strong. Won't happen.

After the Q&A they take us down to the cancer centre, the McDermott Unit. It's a modular prefabricated building (i.e. like a big porta cabin) – the type they built never intending it to be permanent, then roll forward 20 years (I'm guessing) and it is. Permanent. We had one at school. We called it the red block. It was a complete tip. Before I even realise it we're in the treatment room. It's not what you'd expect, there is a square-shaped nurse's station in the middle of the room that looks like another reception desk, but it isn't. It's the nerve centre of the chemo treatment room. The building isn't quite a square, more of a fat rectangle. There are five treatment chairs down each of the longer sides. They're not normal chairs. They are medical-type recliner chairs. Next to each chair is some sort of machinery and a stand with drips on it. All the chairs are blue. Except one in the corner. It's green.

Catherine has shown me video clips on YouTube so I know about the 'communal' treatment but it's so weird. You would think you get your chemo in a private room with nobody else watching. But apparently not. There's curtains which they can pull round if needed. It's a bit like a lap dancing club in that way. You get in the back room and then end up slightly disappointed by the lack of privacy.

I think my misconception, though, is all about the treatment. I didn't think it was just injections and drips. I assumed it was something much more invasive which required that greater degree of privacy. Until a few weeks ago I honestly thought that chemo involved some sort of brain surgery. I thought they would need to open up my head with a knife and mess about with things. Learning that it's just an injection (okay, more than one) makes it all less daunting. I've had injections before. I can do this, no bother.

Thursday 20 March 2014

I'm in work when my mobile rings. It's a nurse from the McDermott Unit. Her accent is Scottish.

'I know you have an appointment at 2.30 this afternoon for your bone marrow biopsy, but is there any chance you can come sooner?'

It's only just after 9am. Why do they want me to come sooner, I wonder?

'What time do you mean?'

'Like, now, or as soon as you can, we'll see you as soon as you get here.'

'Okay, I'm coming now.'

What the fuck is this about? I lock my laptop and leave work immediately. As I drive to the hospital my mind starts to race. This isn't for a bone marrow biopsy. This is something else. They've told me to come immediately. I had a load of blood tests less than two days ago. They've found something. Is it more spread than they thought? Oh shit. It's HIV. Now it all makes sense. The nurse taking the blood samples made a special point about the HIV one. For no reason, like. And then Dr Ong basically acted like I had it. I have got H I fucking V. Just brilliant.

I can't though, can I? Could I? Fuck, there was that one time a few years back on our Jim's stag do in Hamburg. It was after midnight and we'd been drinking for hours. I got separated from the rest of the group. I staggered into an establishment of ill repute … and there were two of them … German girls … must be early 20s … good looking (I think) … they made a beeline for me … must have seen me coming.

I remember one of them staring into my eyes and in that clipped German English saying to me, 'Do you want it?'

I was so pissed I just couldn't say no to her and got stuck right in.

Now, as it happens, the establishment was Kentucky Fried Chicken and what the girls were offering me was their half-eaten bucket of chicken. But still, that can't be great hygiene. And some of the pubs I've drunk in, and the bogs I've used (when drunk mainly) – I'm sure some of the toilet seats I have sat on have been infected with HIV.

I get to the Ulster and there is a queue for the car park. At least I don't have to pay. I phone my wife and explain the situation.

'I bet I've got fucking HIV, I bet that's what it is.'

'Don't be silly, you can't have HIV.'

'They fucking told me, the doctors did, they told me I can't have fucking cancer, and I do. So what's the difference? I've probably got HIV as well.'

If when I get there it's Dr Ong I'm in trouble. They'd get the big guns out for HIV.

I wait. Why am I waiting? Come on and tell me, get this done. I feel like I'm waiting for test results now. This is what it feels like. And it's going to be bad. I just know it now.

Joanne appears from the corridor that runs by the waiting room. She calls me forward. She's smiling. Not funny Joanne. Not fucking funny.

She's taking me to one of the rooms. If Dr Ong is in there I'm completely screwed.

But Dr Ong isn't there. So who is this? A junior doctor, oncologist, as Joanne explains. She hasn't done this procedure before. Do I mind if she does it?

Procedure? What procedure? Oh, the bone marrow biopsy? We're really here for a bone marrow biopsy and I haven't got HIV? Oh thank the lord. Of course she can do it, she can do whatever she wants to me. Oh fantastic.

'Yeah course, everybody has got to learn,' I say like a jolly punter allowing a new bar maid to pull his pint.

They told me a bit about this procedure the other day. Apparently it's a two-minute job, needle into the lower back, a bit like taking blood, only they're taking bone marrow.

What even is bone marrow? Come to think of it, what the fuck is marrow? Marrowfat peas? Do dogs eat marrow? Anyway, they want some of it from me and, like all these checks, I'm happy enough.

They know what they're doing.

They offered me sedation earlier in the week but said it wasn't really necessary as there would be a local anaesthetic. Sure, sounds grand. So I've gone to work and driven up. I'm wearing a suit but I take off the jacket.

As they are doing the pre-procedure prep, I realise that the junior doc is actually a bit of an dick. My reason for this is the way she's trying to reinforce the hierarchy between herself and Joanne. And I like Joanne. It's only one sentence but it's enough – I can't even work out what they're doing as I'm face down on the bed (i.e. back upwards) – 'You do the nursey bit; I'll do the doctor bit.'

You just called her nursey – you patronising wee bitch.

My opinion of Dr Jr worsens. She puts the needle into me to take the sample and for a split second I'm paralysed head to toe in the most excruciating pain I have ever felt in my whole 32 and a half years of life. It is torture, this is what torture is. A thin metal rod being slowly and firmly shoved into my spine. She takes the needle out. Well I'm glad that's over.

I hear them talking. Joanne's telling her she hasn't got it, the bone marrow.

She goes again. And again she's killing me. I realise that I'm biting my arm. Hard. My white shirt is turning grey. I am soaked in sweat.

She abandons.

Joanne, nursey, then takes over. I want to scream so badly. Let it all out. But I can't. I feel the hairs of my arm in my mouth and my teeth in my arm.

I don't look up, but realise that my old friend Dr Alshoufi has joined the party.

Joanne tries again and shows him the difficulty she's having.

'I can't lock on,' she explains. Lock on? This is all a bit less pleasant than I was expecting.

Joanne brings me a cup of water. It's down my throat and sweated back out of the pores of my body in an instant. She brings me another.

Soon, Dr Alshoufi is having a turn. I'm not making any external noise but they can tell from my body spasms and heat and redness that I am in considerable pain.

'We'll have to sedate him,' he declares.

'We can't do, he's driven,' Joanne tells him.

Dr Jr is hiding in the corner now. Her voice is the most distant as Joanne and Dr Alshoufi take turns on me. I can't tell who is doing what.

A mobile phone rings. Dr Alshoufi answers it. I can tell that it's a personal call. He seems to be negotiating rent on a flat. But he's very near to me.

'He's not on the phone while he's doing this, is he?' I ask out loud.

Joanne confirms that it's her dishing out the punishment for now.

'I'll call you later', Dr Alshoufi tells the person on the phone. 'I'm doing a procedure. It's not nice.'

No it's not nice, is it? It's actually awful. Eventually, between them, Joanne and Dr Alshoufi get whatever they need from me out of my back. I turn over and sit up on the bed on my elbows, sipping another cup of water. Joanne is patting my forehead with a cold damp cloth. I am shattered.

Dr Alshoufi walks towards me with a piece of paper in his hand.

'We need to get a certain number of these completed. Would you mind filling this in?'

He drops the paper on my chest.

It takes me a few seconds to register, but he has just handed me a feedback form. Feedback form? The world has gone mad. My body spasms again but this time I'm crying with laughter so much that the bed is shaking. You couldn't make this up. I give them full marks just for the hell of it.

Friday 21 February 2014

The purpose of this heart scan is to check the condition of my heart so that they know it's safe to give me the chemo. I don't know the detail but the gist of it is that it can mess you up, so if you've a dodgy ticker they need to know. They have used the word 'echo' to describe this procedure. I have no idea why and haven't questioned it. It's just another of those things to tick off the list. It cannot possibly do me any harm.

The worst outcome from this is that I have a bad heart. But surely it would be useful to know that, wouldn't it? It's the same with all this testing. It's diagnostic. It's bad to be ill. But good to know that you are ill; because if you don't know then you can't get better.

I'm assuming my heart is in good condition, but you never know.

I'd not seen much of Burnley playing Southampton as they'd been in the top flight for as long as I could remember, but they'd been relegated at the end of 2004/05. If you're from Burnley, somewhere as far south as Southampton (and it has the word 'south' in it even) is pretty damn exotic, so a group of around eight of us, all lads between 21 and 25, had decided to make a weekend of it in December 2005. It was like a stag do but there was no wedding. Perfect.

We set off nice and early. If you're having a pint at Manchester T3 before you're normally awake then you know you're in for a good day. We were drinking at the Christmas market in Southampton town centre by about 10am, and by 11am one of us had disturbed an elderly lady (about 80 years old, give or take) using the toilet in a nearby Starbucks. Standard stuff.

It's all a bit blurry. We had what felt like a long walk to the St Mary's stadium, we went 1-0 down but equalised late on through Ade Akinbiyi and we all went mental. We had some good banter with the Southampton fans outside the ground, which threatened to get a bit tastier but nothing came of it, and we carried on afterwards and landed in the hotel in the early hours. Just a great day out at the seaside. We didn't see the sea though.

The next day, coming back from the airport driving back up the M66, a sinking feeling came over me. Right in the pit of my stomach. Somersaulting.

I didn't want to go home. My heart was hurting.

I'm back at the Ulster Hospital again. I'm here with such frequency it's beginning to feel like a client site or something. Just another industrial building in which people do stuff. Albeit I'm here in a different capacity – I'm somebody that stuff is being done to.

My job is a bit strange. We don't do tangible things. It's professional advice that might help somebody else doing intangible things which eventually, down the line, might affect somebody doing tangible stuff, but it's pretty intangible. I visit clients and I see people actually making stuff. Real things. It must be nice to make a difference.

These hospitals though are an extreme; you can't get more tangible. It's people doing things to people. Proper real world outcomes. It's applied life sciences 24/7.

I'm in another part of the hospital that I've not been in before and it's a shithole. The Ulster is a collection of bits that have been rebuilt recently, which are nice, and bits that haven't which are grim, but are earmarked for development. I get to a reception desk in a room no bigger than 12 x 12ft. It's like a scene from an Egyptian street market. There are about 25 people in the room; it's bursting and noisy. I'm half expecting to see a bird in a cage swinging from the ceiling.

I tell the lad on reception what I'm here for and he directs me down a corridor into another waiting room. The contrast between the two waiting rooms is so severe you would honestly think somebody is taking the piss. For a start, I've transitioned into a new (i.e. shiny) part of the hospital. The biggest difference though is the sheer space. This room is at least six times the size of the last one, but, aside from the female receptionist, there are only two other people in the room. It's a couple, must be in their 50s. I've only been sat down a minute when a nurse appears and calls for 'Maureen Brown'. Nobody moves.

Another nurse, she looks about 15 years old, walks past. She is carrying a share bag of Cadbury's Giant Buttons. I hope she is going to share those. She goes on.

A few minutes later nurse number one returns and again asks for 'Maureen Brown'. I'm slightly puzzled. It's not hard to work out that there are only three people in the room, two of which are blokes, and the only female has already declared herself not to be Maureen Brown. The situation hasn't changed in the last four minutes. I start to wonder what part of the hospital I've walked into. Is it some sort of training centre for 'development' nurses? Or is it the patients? Am I on the loony ward? Am I imagining the whole thing?

A couple of minutes pass and the same nurse is back again asking for Maureen Brown, but there are still no additional people in the room. I'm half expecting Jeremy Beadle to pop out but he can't because he's dead, and I'm trying to find a fellow soul to lock eyes of bewilderment with and shrug shoulders at this utter craziness, but I can't because there are hardly any people in the room. At this point the female of the couple pipes up and explains that she is called Maureen, but not Maureen Brown. Her name is Maureen Smith. That's fine, I'm thinking, you're not Maureen Brown and there is enough difference between Smith and Brown.

The nurse looks at her clipboard and says, 'That'll do, come this way.'

That'll do, that'll fucking do! What have I just witnessed? Has that really taken ten minutes? No wonder the other waiting room resembles a Nairobi zoo. Half the people in there are meant to be somewhere else.

I'm still laughing to myself when Button girl appears (without the Buttons). She has her clipboard. You've got to be kidding me. I'm the only person left so it has to me, but, nevertheless, she screws up her face as though she's looking at photographs of dogshit, and attempts to pronounce my surname.

'Michael Henk.'

That's it, if it's too hard for you then miss half the letters out, that'll do the trick.

She's so much younger than me, but I'm the patient. It didn't used to be like this. Since the age of 18, I've seen a doctor or medical professional maybe a half dozen times. They're older than me. Wiser. Know their stuff. How is this wee 'slip of a girl' going to tell me anything about my heart?

She asks me to take my top off and lie on the bed. It barely feels legal. Then she introduces the cold jelly. I look at the machinery. I see the GE logo. I've been here before. Have

I? There's a real familiarity about this, I'm thinking, as she hovers the device over and around my chest and we watch the black and white image on the screen beside the bed.

'Is this a baby scanner?' I ask her.

She looks at me as though I'm insane.

'Because it looks just the same as those. You know, those baby scanning machines.'

'No,' she says. 'I don't know what you mean, I've never seen one of those.'

'Well,' I tell her, 'you have, it's pretty much that.'

The accountant in me is constantly judging the NHS and the craziness of it and trying to think of ways to make it better. My idea as I'm sat there on the bed is for some sort of transaction. A merger. Yes, a merger between the baby scanners and the heart scanners. That's a great idea. Might be a few teething problems – the baby scanner people won't be able to read the heart scan, and vice versa you'd have a similar problem. You can see it now actually – wee baby Matilda pops out with a third leg and she's a boy because the heart scanner (Button girl maybe) didn't know what she was doing. Okay then, perhaps they could train together, because the machines are the same and they must need to be trained on how to use the machines. And the gel, it's got to be the same gel. But you'll still have that issue on interpretation that has to be part of the training. Well, I'm thinking one room on how to operate the machine (baby scanners and heart scanners mixed in together, bit of banter and cross-team working, love all that), and then part two they go into separate rooms to learn interpretation. No actually, maintenance, that's where it is – it's the same guy who comes around and fixes the machines, because it's the same machine. Yes, that's the synergy. Although they might already have one person? Could it even be subcontracted to a third party? I'm assuming it is but it might not even be the same machine.

Actually, just leave it as it is. It's grand, brilliant NHS. Can't beat it.

'Oh look, I can see a foot,' I say, attempting a joke and thinking it's funny.

She gives me a look of pity, like I'm a dad who is trying too hard to impress the teenagers.

'How does it look?' I ask her as she reviews the computer at the other side of the room.

'Yeah, normal,' she says. 'I'll have to do a report … but all looks normal. Why are you having a heart scan anyway? Do you know?'

Well, err, yeah, I know why I am here, I'd have thought that was a given. But surely she has some notes that provide some sort of context for her. If not, she could put her foot in it. Perhaps tell a cancer joke. Are there cancer jokes even? I don't know any.

'I've got cancer.'

'Have you? You don't look like you've got cancer …'

'Look here …' I point to my neck. Even though I've had the biopsy the lump is getting bigger. It's bigger than it's ever been.

She now can't help but notice it. I'm getting this look a lot. Especially from females. They think they're talking to some normal average chap only to realise it's the elephant man.

'Oh my god.' Indeed button girl, 'oh my god' indeed.

Saturday 22 March 2014
Charlton v Burnley

It's been an eventful week. Just a week since the Leeds game but it feels like ages ago. I've only done a few things but it's all stuff I've never done before where I can't even imagine what it's like before I'm in the thick of it. When the days are like that they last for years.

Now then. For my trouble I think the least I'm due is another three points. Please, Lord, are you listening to this? It all feels aligned. Clarets on course for promotion. And, finally, I'm heading for beating this cancer. Fair enough, I've not started that phase yet. I've another nine days to go. Can't wait, bring it on. But I'm doing the groundwork. The absolute necessaries that we'll build the rest from.

To be fair, it's not dissimilar to Dyche and Burnley. He took over from Eddie Howe in November 2012 and, results-wise, didn't exactly set the world alight in 2012/13. In fact, at one point we looked like we could even go down – it bunched up, which can happen in the Championship. But what he was doing was building the foundation. The mindset. The culture. The ethos. The mentality. This season. Wow. A lot of managers don't get the chance to even attempt to do that. That's another great thing about Burnley. We aren't trigger-happy when it comes to managers. Not like last week's opponents.

Charlton are yet another team, who, when I started getting into football in the 1980s, were in the First Division. I remember them from the Football '87 album. It was the first album I completed and the first I started. I've embarked upon several since, but most of the time I didn't finish. The World Cup 1990 Orbis ring binder type was the exception.

The really annoying thing about Football '87 is that I went about 25 years thinking I had finished it. But I hadn't. Kevin Gage – why the fuck did I put you in twice? Next to yourself? What was I playing at? We were at my mum and dad's house last year and I was proudly showing George the first of my two completed football albums. We'd got to Wimbledon so we were nearly done. He's thinking who? And it's the last First Division team, and then I spot it. Two Kevin Gage and zero John Kay. To make it worse, George had a drink of blackcurrant juice which was getting a bit too close to my treasured album. I was too focused on him not spilling juice to notice two little hands (this is two-year-old Sam now) tearing a chunk (circa one third) off the front cover. It had gone downhill quickly. Only five minutes ago I was showing off my treasured piece of football memorabilia. Now it was incomplete and its cover was hanging off. Life can change fast. I repatriated it to NI the next day.

My nanna helped me with it. She bought me stickers all the time, and I remember the Sunday she took me to her friend's house to 'acquire' some swaps. An 11-year-old lived there but I didn't see him. He was still in bed. His mum shouted up to him:

'David, Winifred (my nanna's name, she hated it) is going to give you a pound (£1) for all your swaps, is that okay?'

'Yeah,' came the one-word reply.

I came away thinking two things. You are so cool to be 11 and in bed and not giving one and replying so nonchalantly with a one-word answer. But also, I've got a steal here – £1 for the biggest stack of swaps (one of those where you can barely get an elastic band round and it's impossible to stop the stack from leaning) I'd ever seen.

Football '87 is a barometer. And George made the observation. It features English Division One, with shorter pages on Division Two and Scottish One and Two. Where are Burnley in this album? Not even nearly there – we were far too near to the bottom of Division Four. And Scottish football – was Scottish Division Two really better than the third and fourth tiers in England?

As for Charlton, they're okay, I don't mind them. I love football grounds. And I love a good football ground story. They've got one and it's beautiful. They'd played at the Valley since 1919, but by the time of my Football '87 album they were ground-sharing with Crystal Palace. I remember an article in *Match/Shoot/90 Minutes* in the late 1980s featuring the Valley – it was an overgrown ruin – covered in weeds and trees, etc. But, and this is the romance, they got back home. Tidied it up, and modernised it. It's not just a club coming back from the brink.

That's normally finances/balance sheet related. Very intangible. A football stadium is a big, monumental cathedral of a thing. The visual of seeing one go derelict but then spring back to life is a thing of sheer beauty.

Danny Ings is still out injured, which makes me slightly nervous about today, just slightly though. I think there's still goals in us, and if we can get one, then that might be enough today. I fancy us for a clean sheet, probably more than I do for a win. Ashley Barnes makes his first Burnley start following his January move from Brighton and steps up to the mark to nod us ahead towards the end of the first half. Lovely. A half-time lead. Even though I'm only following the game on Sky Sports News I know there's only one outcome now. Vokesy slams in a penalty early in the second half and substitute Kightly scores a deflected goal in injury time. 3-0 Burnley. A casual away win in the capital. Dyche is making this look easy. All in our stride. That's what I'm about too. Me and Sean, we're kindred spirits.

Monday 24 March 2014

I take a call from Dr Ong. The multidisciplinary team have discussed me again (I feel special just hearing that, lol – I get a bit of a glow).

They're adamant now that I should have 6 x RCHOP. Maybe some radiotherapy, maybe not.

I'm pleased. Not that I love chemo and want double, I've never even tried it. I'm just glad for the clarity. I'm also glad that I don't have to decide. I want the professionals to do that bit and thankfully now they have.

I tell Catherine. She reacts differently. She wants to know why. I tell her, 'Well that's what the multidisciplinary team have decided is best.'

'Well, why do they think that is best?'

'Well I don't know, it must be due to reasons of science and medicine. I don't fucking know.'

'Did you not ask?'

'No.'

'What? Why did you not ask them?'

'Why does it matter?'

'Why does it matter? Do you not want to know?'

'Well I probably won't understand it anyway. Who am I to challenge them? They were on the fence with three or six. That was a bit frustrating. And now they've thought more and are saying six. For definite. That's good.'

Tuesday 25 March 2014
Burnley v Doncaster

These are the banana skins. The home games where you're nailed on to win. Typical Burnley to balls it up.

I think it was Stan Ternent who first started using that phrase, banana skin. 1999/2000 was going well under Stan Ternent. After stabilising the club/sorting out the Waddle mess in 1998/99, we were now looking upwards.

Results were going well, and so was the manner of a lot of them. It was sometimes Manchester United-esque how we seemed to get results from difficult situations.

The last game of the century was one of those. Oxford United at home. We were 1-0 down and then 2-1 down as late as the 80th minute, until Andy Payton equalised. Shooting towards the Jimmy Mc Lower, you just knew it was going to happen for us, and sure enough, in the last minute, Payton popped up again to complete his hat-trick and give us a 3-2 win.

As soon as I got home, as ever, I got straight on to Teletext to see how all the other English league matches had finished. One result in particular stood out; Cardiff had snatched an injury-time equaliser at Blackpool. That was interesting. I took my Coral betting slip out of my pocket to check what I was thinking. Yes, I had backed that game for a draw on one of my accumulators.

There was (and still is) a Coral shop opposite Turf Moor and I would normally nip in before kick-off and put a few football accumulators on – £1 or £2 stakes per line, and never spending more than a fiver in total. I always did it in a rush between the pub and getting into the ground. The slip in my hand was time stamped at 14.54 – it probably took me less than one minute to decide what I was doing. I could normally only half-remember what I had backed because I took so little time over it and was always at least semi-intoxicated.

But I had initially thought I had got the Blackpool–Cardiff match wrong. I hadn't. I looked at the rest of that line – it was a £1 stake on a tenfold accumulator – a mixture of homes, aways and a single draw. At least I had the draw right. I was recollecting the scores that I'd heard coming out the ground over the tannoy and in the car on the radio and thinking I have a lot of these right, which do I have wrong? I flicked around on Teletext looking at each division where I had backed something and waited agonisingly for the page to move from 1/3 to 2/3 to 3/3.

It took me about 15 minutes to be confident that I had all ten results right. My £1 stake was getting me back £732. I don't know how people feel when they're checking correct lottery numbers, but I was absolutely buzzing. Not just at my luck, but, so I convinced myself, at my talent, my footballing ability, my nous and knowledge of the game. Far better than winning the lottery.

I was an 18-year-old student at the time. I wasn't living in poverty by any stretch but was pretty lean with the old finances. £732! I could buy a load of beer (and cider as well) with that!

It was good fun lifting the cash from Coral the next day. The bloke on the counter had it all set aside for me. He smiled and shook his head. 'You'll never do that again,' he said. Naively I thought he was talking crap. It remains my biggest ever betting victory, despite another 14 years of gambling and many much, much higher stakes.

I'm not sure Sean Dyche knows what a banana skin is. He probably just eats the whole banana without even noticing it.

We don't do banana skins. Not with Sean in charge. He won't let the lads get carried away. It's all more composed and calm, and relentless at the same time.

Relentless. Relentless. I want to be relentless. Chase it down. Every lost ball. Press. Press. I will never ever give in. Fucking never. Come on. I want to be the best ever cancer patient. Ever, in the whole fucking world. I'm going to pursue that goal. Relentlessly.

Doncaster are here for a point and you can't blame them; taking that from Turf Moor on a wet and miserable night is not to be sniffed at. Half-time comes and goes and it's 0-0 and the nerves are on their way. Being at the top of the league is stressful. Any dropped points feel like defeats. Especially at home, especially against a team from the bottom half of the table. Just into the second half, we get a soft penalty (you get the luck at the top as well) which Vokesy blasts into the top corner. Euphoria. Relief. I'll have a cup of tea to celebrate. Not just the goal. I'll celebrate the fact that I know I can enjoy the rest of the night. Because we're going to win. With a quarter of an hour to go, Stanislas goes one on one and drills the ball past the Donny keeper to seal it.

Friday 28 March 2014

So before they nuke my bollocks next week I've hastily arranged a last-minute appointment at the fertility clinic, or, for my purpose, the 'wank bank'. That's right, they're going to store this stuff for the next 20 years. I don't know where they'll keep it. I'm picturing some sort of underground vault with a wall of mini drawers, like small safes, and you need a medieval-looking key to unlock it, and inside there is a golden capsule with my semen in it. Yummy.

I have no idea whether my 'family is complete' but there hasn't been time to decide so I guess I might as well. I can think of worse things to do on a Friday morning.

Well, you would forgive me for thinking that. It's all about expectation and I think in my head I have an image of a fertility clinic from an American film in a shiny private medical centre, where the receptionist is a stunner, and even offers to give you a hand.

They didn't tell me about the form filling in. It is sheer lunacy. A middle-aged bald bloke talks me through it – there must be 30 different forms that require my signature and I have wanker's cramp in my right arm before I've even started. The nurse then leads me to the 'room' (I say room but it is more of a dungeon) and hands me a pot. This is where it gets really tough. I was expecting something a bit wider that I could actually aim into easily with no mess guaranteed. This thing is narrow. It is going to be tricky.

There's a black box file on the table with the 'material'. I open it and am disappointed to find there is only a single magazine; Playboy from a couple of years ago. I flick through it, but very briefly. Once I realise that around half the pages are stuck together I hastily return it to the box.

I can't get comfy in the chair. I stand up instead. I hear a commotion coming from the street outside. The room I'm in is a basement with a frosted glass window up high which is just at street level. I can't see through the windows but I think the room must be next to either a smoking shelter or a bus stop. Either way, the soundtrack to my 'session' is the whines of a West Belfast woman and her man problems. Eventually I get there.

My trauma isn't quite finished. Rather than leave the sample in the room I now have to find the nurse and hand it to her (yes, my hand to her hand). Lovely.

'Oh yes, that's plenty,' she says.

Good job. Keep some for yourself if you want love. I drive back to work. I laugh to myself. I'll enjoy telling this one.

Saturday 29 March 2014
Burnley v Leicester

Second versus first in the league. Win this game and we're chasing Leicester down. I'm hesitant though. One word. Nugent.

Dave Nugent scores goals against Burnley. It's as simple as that. He's also scored a few for us during a loan spell in 2009/10 but, generally speaking, when I hear the word Nugent I think, 'oh shit'. He played for Preston for a number of years and always seemed to score against us. He tainted my memories of playing Preston in some ways, just as David Healey had done a few years earlier.

My first away game watching the Clarets was against Preston, at Deepdale, in the second leg of the Sherpa Van Trophy in 1988. We were a win away from Wembley. And we were rare visitors, having played there only twice before, in losing FA Cup finals in 1947 and 1962. But Preston, or Nob End as I would later call them, were a division above us and strong favourites to win.

There were thousands of Burnley fans crammed into the terrace behind the goal and a few hundred more seated in the adjacent stand, which is where we were sat. Me, our Jim, my dad, his mate Dave (Uncle) and his son Matthew. I can't remember if the stand was wooden or not, but the seats were definitely wood. Not even seats, they were benches with a line of paint to mark out the boundary of where your arse is meant to be. They don't do seats like these anymore, and they are certainty prone to encroachment. I ended up with around 10cm of space, which was more than enough for six-year-old me.

I didn't have a great view of the match, although above the high heads in front of me I could see a block of green at the far end of the pitch, the end opposite the Burnley fans. That meant I did see as George Oghani broke free in the first half to put Burnley 1-0 ahead against the run of play, play which I hadn't been able to see. At the same end, Preston equalised midway through the second half to take the game into extra time, a concept I wasn't too familiar with. I was learning on the job.

No sooner had extra time started than everybody around me and in the terrace to my right erupted in celebration. We'd scored to take the lead again, but I saw nothing as Ashley Hoskin lashed the ball into the net right in front of the Burnley fans. With a few minutes of extra time remaining, a roar of expectation went up from the Burnley fans, as, unbeknown to me, we launched a counter attack with Preston pressing. I soon learnt why, as into the green block that I could see strode George Oghani, who squared the ball to Paul Comstive to fire home for 3-1 to Burnley.

'Wem-ber-lee, Wem-ber-lee, we're the famous Burnley FC and we're going to Wem-ber-lee,' went the chant from the Burnley fans as I learnt a new song, and one which I would sing very rarely over the years that followed. The Burnley players, staff and fans were ecstatic, and I didn't need to be told that this was massive. I could see it right in front of me. Everywhere. Sheer jubilation.

It was my first season watching the Clarets and it was going to finish with a trip to Wembley. Even at age six I knew about Wembley, it was some mythical place where they played the cup final. And it was massive and had semi-circles behind the goals. And the pitch was bigger. And the goals were perfect with those big green stanchions on the back of them.

Only a year earlier Burnley had almost been relegated from the Football League. What a turnaround.

On the way home we stopped at a pub on the outskirts of Preston. We were in a different town but you wouldn't have known – Burnley fans were milling about everywhere. Me, our Jim and Matthew stayed in my Uncle Dave's car whilst our dads took turns to come out to check on us and ply us with Coca Cola (glass bottles with a straw) and Salt n Vinegar Seabrook crisps. It was a school night. I was six. It was the best night out I'd ever had.

Oghani was top scorer for us in my first season watching the Clarets, and he became an immediate hero for me. This was despite him being, let's just say, a bit of a character, most famous for what we call the 'ironing board incident'.

The incident had definitely occurred before the Wembley trip, because some fans had T-shirts with a cartoon image of George holding an ironing board in surfer-style pose. I assume they were not produced by the club shop but you never know.

It's hard to work out the true story, but the most sense you can make of it is something like this …

The location is Asda, Longsight, Manchester. George Oghani is buying an ironing board but 'forgets' to pay for a bag of screws (or could have been window bolts). A security guard challenges him. So George hits him with the nearest thing, which is the said ironing board. He was arrested and charged with assault. What? Don't all professional footballers do that? Pretty standard? I wonder how many of the current Burnley squad have ever bought an ironing board in Asda? I wonder how many of them even step foot in Asda?

But it all just added to the flavour of the man. Another reason I liked him was because he was black (well, mixed race). There was a novelty thing about that; all of the other Burnley players were white. And as a town, you just don't see many black people in Burnley. So yes, I liked him partly because he was black. Is that racist? No, I don't think so.

When, in the spring of 1989, I had to choose a confirm-ation name (Catholic thing, a bit weird to be honest) there was only one contender. It had to be George.

Only about a month after that, he was sacked by Burnley after a training ground bust up with goalkeeper Chris Pearce. Pearce came off worse by all accounts, and stayed with the club until 1992. Oghani was the guilty party, with the fight rumoured to have occurred because (i) Oghani was robbing from players' clothes in the changing room or (ii) Oghani had broken into Pearce's car or (iii) Oghani was shagging Pearce's wife. It was probably one of the first two; your modern footballer would only be interested in the third.

I'd bonded with the name though by that stage. I gave the name to my first son. He probably thinks he's named after the patron saint of our fine country. George, mate, I'm sorry pal, you're named after a goalkeeper-battering, window-lock thieving, ironing board 'using' journeyman striker who once played for Hyde. Oh George Oghani! Oh George Oghani!

The game is live on Sky but I get caught up in traffic and don't get back into the house until 12.25pm. We're ten minutes in. I'm pleased to see it's 0-0. I'm less pleased that I can't see Vokesy on the pitch. Not sure what Sean is playing at here. Gradually, the commentators clarify things for me – Vokesy has gone off due to an injury. So we're playing just Ashley Barnes up front. Bugger. I hope it's not a bad one. Ings and Vokes out at the same time would be a disaster. We move to a 4-5-1 formation for the first time all season, out of necessity rather than choice.

Leicester have started with that man Dave Nugent up front, and he's partnered by another English striker who I've never heard of before this season but seems to be pretty decent, called Jamie Vardy. The latter gets injured just after the half hour. Leicester have more money and options than us, so Vardy is replaced with another striker, New Zealand's Chris Wood. If he's from New Zealand he can't be up to much I think, he's probably better at chasing sheep than defenders. He should probably be playing for Leeds.

It doesn't take him long to prove me wrong. About a minute in fact. He powers through the Burnley defence and lays the ball off to that man, or should I say, that fucker,

Nugent, who curls it into the corner beyond Tom Heaton. 1-0 to Leicester.

I worry we won't have a goal in us, not with these injuries.

There is another goal in the game, but sadly not for us. With about ten to go, the substitute Wood attempts an audacious lob and the ball soars over Heaton before dropping into the net. It hurts. My first defeat since cancer came. God, I thought we had a deal here, what are you playing at?

Sunday 30 March 2014

It's Mother's day, one day until my cup final. I'm not even going to drink today. I want to be at the peak of my powers.

My wife has her mum and dad round. Combine them with two more adults, two kids and two cats and it gets noisy very quickly. A bit like a zoo but with only two official animals.

I don't quite hear the phone ringing. We never use the land line, and by the time I've registered it's ringing it has stopped. I realise my mobile isn't in my pocket. I locate it in the kitchen. There are three missed calls from my mum. There is a voicemail.

I don't need to hear it to know. It's my nanna. My lovely wee nanna. She's gone.

Part Four

ONWARDS AND UPWARDS

Monday 31 March 2014
Me v Chemo One

Not exactly the weekend I'd been hoping for. Defeat against our promotion rivals and my nanna is dead.

Well then. Right. Here we fucking go. Let's knock ten bells of shit out of this. I'm not fighting though. The chemo is. The chemo is fighting the cancer. Not me. I've just got to do what I can to give the chemo the best possible chance. Be the best I can be. The best patient. Ultimately, I can't have any control over what actually happens out there on the field. I'm not playing. I really am just like Dyche. He gets the players ready. Prepares meticulously; no stone unturned, every last detail. But when the players cross the white line it's out of his hands. And mine too.

My wife has come with me to the hospital but we both question the wisdom. She doesn't do well with blood, needles, and hospitals. She's squeamish. And she finds all of this stuff scary. We've argued a fair bit. We've got very different styles. She's risk averse and wants to protect against the worst happening.

She wants to scenario plan. I'm positive to the verge of being in denial. When she talked about bringing a bed downstairs and putting it in the study I just flipped. I completely lost my rag. She thinks she's preparing now because in a few weeks' time I won't have the energy to move a bed. I think she's writing me off and trying to dampen my positivity. There is only one reason I sleep downstairs, and it's because I get too pissed.

She says I won't talk to her about it. I've told her already, if she wants to have a negative/worst case scenario discussion she needs to have it with somebody else. I'm not having that discussion. I will not, in any circumstances, entertain any form of negative thinking. She says it's being realistic. I disagree, it's pessimism rather than realism. I don't want to be exposed to those thoughts. I fully believe that negativity alone can kill a man.

I mean, just look at Dyche. I'm living by his lead right now. We absolutely have to believe we will win. And I'll do my best to make sure it happens.

I'm called in not much later than 8.30am as scheduled and told to pick a chair. I know what I want thanks to the open day. I take the outlier green chair in the corner. A nurse comes to take my bloods. She tells me that this is what they'll do at every chemo treatment – check my bloods first to make sure that I'm okay to have the chemo.

I think these hospitals, when in full flight, are just amazing. The bloods I have taken are collected by boys with trolleys who take them to a lab. The lab analyses the samples and logs the results. Within about 45 minutes the nurse comes back. We're good to go.

The first thing in my RCHOP cocktail is rituximab. My wife knows all about this. I don't. It's not a chemotherapy drug. It's something they put into you first. It's on a drip. So it's slow to administer, not like an injection. The nurse explains it to me. The R goes into me and puts down markers or flags to help the chemo to know where to go. It sounds like a fucking treasure hunt. It's a relativity new drug, the treatment used to just be called CHOP. But the R makes it much more effective. Give it to me.

But the R isn't great. It can make you sick, tired, nauseous, etc., so they tell me anyway. And it will take about four hours to administer. They'll start it slowly and every 30 minutes or so check my temperature and blood pressure and if all is okay they'll speed it up. Four hours is on the basis that they will speed me up every 30 minutes. It could take much longer.

Mary does most of this for me. It's a bit boring being stuck in a chair for that long. You can get up to go to the toilet but you've got to unplug the monitor and bring the drip, complete with its stand, with you. And you need to make sure you don't accidentally knock the cannula out of your arm because that wouldn't be good. So it's a ballache.

Very similar to being on a plane when you can't be arsed going because of the need to play musical chairs with the person next to you.

Catherine is not enjoying this. She keeps nipping out to do stuff. Smoking, I assume. And she keeps wanting to know if I want anything from the hospital shop. Well unless they sell cans of Red Stripe then probably not.

After 30 minutes Mary comes to check on me. My temperature and heart are okay. She asks if I feel any sickness or nausea. I don't. She speeds up the dosage. It's my first test is this and I'm glad that I've passed it. There is still a load of this R stuff to go; if we don't speed up I'll be here all night.

Mary tells me that if they can speed it up every 30 minutes today, then next time I'll qualify for rapid infusion. What this means is that they'll go full speed from the off and it will take more like one and a half hours instead of four. Well that's something worth doing if I can. I make a mental note to tell them I'm feeling fine every time they ask. It's the one-game-at-a-time mantra – win today, and deal with the next match when it comes.

The old dear next to me is on her first cycle of treatment too, and she's also being given R at the same time as me.

After an hour or so I realise that she's not flying through it and they're not speeding her up.

Because I know she's on the same treatment, I intentionally eavesdrop on her conversations with the nurses. There's one chat which I think I must have misheard so I ask the nurse to clarify it.

'Mary, I just heard you there ... what was that you were saying ... about alcohol?'

Alcohol is my biggest weakness. I drink too much. I always have. I started too early. I do worry that in some way my drinking led me here.

'If you drink ... do you drink?'

'Yes ... I have been known to enjoy the odd one.'

She knows from my tone and expression that I've just delivered the understatement of the decade.

'Well, what we find with patients that drink ... they don't tend to have much sickness from chemo ... non-drinkers do though.'

Blimey. All my years of alcohol abuse are finally vindicated. I always knew I was doing the right thing. I was built for this.

'So, should the non-drinkers not start drinking?' I ask her. 'Plus, they might enjoy it.'

There's a large whiteboard on the wall just to my left. The whole day is mapped out in black marker. My name is on it. Wow, I feel famous. And they've spelt it correctly as well. That's nice.

Even though the same nurse comes by every 30 minutes, she has to ask me my name and address each time. Even though I'm one of only ten to 12 patients in the room and I haven't moved my arse all morning. And she's the same nurse. It will be risk management of some sort. Some NHS hospital (or health trust, what even is a health trust? Where did that expression come from?) must have been sued for giving the wrong drugs to somebody. So I understand it to some extent, but when she's saying, 'Right Michael, can you tell me your name?' it is a bit farcical, like, it's hardly going to be 'Dave' is it?

I finally stretch the legs and relieve my bladder. I've been drinking water all day. There is a jug next to me which they keep re-filling and there isn't much else to do so I sup it. Drink water, look around, and take it all in. I've brought a book with me but I barely open it. I have my phone but it's a Blackberry and I'm not active on social media.

The toilet is on the far side of the room from where I'm sat. It's a single door straight into a single cubicle. Unisex, disabled friendly. I open the door. It's not a pretty sight. No problems with the cleanliness of the place. No, it's the 80-odd-year-old man having a dump staring back at me that is. I apologise and close the door. In fairness I have no need to apologise. All I did was open an unlocked door. Which, if he didn't want anybody to walk in, he probably should have locked.

I always find the way old folk dress is a funny one. It's all shirt, and ties but for no reason. My nanna's husband (my nanna, I can't believe she's dead), Terry, is a classic one for this. He gets up, has a shower, and then puts on his shirt, tie, trousers and shoes. And then he doesn't even leave the house. He sits there reading the paper, dressed up as a fucking 1980s accountant. If I'm not going out anywhere I wander round the house like a caveman. I wonder if that will change when I get older? When I'm 85 (I'm getting there, there's no doubt about that) will I shirt and tie it or will I be running round the house bollock naked still?

Anyway, the old timer sat on the toilet, he's wearing the classic grey slacks, burgundy v-neck 'sweater', with a shirt and tie popping out the top. It doesn't look that smart though when the slacks are round the ankles and you're curling one out. He should definitely have locked the door.

A nurse asks me if I would like some lunch so I accept the offer. Not the best decision I've ever made. There is a slice of wheaten bread, a portion of butter and a small packet of cheese. That's the highlight. The cup of soup that comes with it is vile. The smell. It's repugnant. It's like a baby has overdosed on pureed vegetables and left their nappy on my tray. I make a mental note to politely decline 'lunch' next time.

When the R is done with, we're on to C, H and O. C is given through a drip but it's not a long one – 30 minutes and we're done. H is different again, it's just two injections. The syringes are chunky though, plenty of liquid in them, so it takes a good ten minutes.

Another nurse comes over and wants to book my next chemo session in my red chemo book. It looks like my homework diary from school. It's a three-week cycle so I'm surprised that the next one is 28 April and not 21 April. Mary tells me it's because 21 April is Easter Monday and they only do blood cancer treatments on a Monday. I'm into NHS operational improvement mode again. I wonder then, what happens the next Monday, will you not have twice as many patients to see? Apparently not, because some are here weekly anyway, but yes they'll be much busier. And is there not risk in delaying treatment of people who need it, for a bank holiday? Mary adds that they would rather work but they can't get enough doctor support to open.

Mary has been doing pretty much all of this but now she's telling me that she'll need to get somebody else for the final one. There's a stand on wheels that they cart about with all the drugs in. There are two more syringes sat on top, big fat ones with a red/orange liquid in them. I can't make up my mind if it looks like Irn Bru. Actually it's more like Tizer. Now there's a drink you don't see often these days. Whatever happened to Tizer? Beechnut chewing gum. Sunkist. Stimorol. All these things were once great and now they're nowhere. Drink it in the su-u-un, Sunkist is the one. Or not anymore. Mary comes back and explains that she isn't qualified to administer this one. It's lethal she tells me, and if it ends up not in your veins it can be trouble. The Perspex packaging has those black and yellow danger type stickers on it. The ones you see on stuff about the house – careful you don't accidentally drink this paint stripper. What is it they're giving me?

Another new nurse, Lisa, a Scottish girl, comes over. She looks at my neck and tells me it's a whopper. I could murder a Burger King right now, I think to myself.

'Hi, is it Dave?' she asks. I recognise the voice as the girl who phoned me the other week – the day I didn't have HIV.

No, I'm not Dave. Lisa explains that the last one is ferocious and that she will be giving it to me. She adds that it will turn my urine red. What?

'Like Tizer colour?'

Rather than wonder what they are putting into me, I think about having red piss. It will only be temporary, like one or two pisses worth, but you have to find the moments of difference and somehow savour them. I've never had red piss before.

Lisa is about to start and then a bloke I've never seen before appears. There are a hell of a lot of people working in the NHS, aren't there? He's a pharmacist, and he wants to explain my take-home medication. From inside the drug trolley he lifts out a massive bag of drugs. It's like when you go to McDonald's (yes I am starving now) and you order so much you get one of those big paper bags with the handles. He sets it on top of the trolley.

One by one he starts lifting out packets of tablets and explaining what it is, when I am to take it and for how many days. It takes a few minutes for me to realise that the bag is all for me; it's been pre-packed in the pharmacy. The P is the easy one, it's a steroid that forms part of the RCHOP and I have one tablet in the hospital now, one tonight and one tomorrow and then no more until the next cycle. The others vary, some are for three days, some for a week, some once a day, some more, some before food, some after. I'm grateful when he hands me an A4 sheet with all this set out. It's a drug timetable. Strangely, I'm thinking wow, is all that for me, all free as well, aren't I lucky?

The pharmacist keeps stressing that it's important that I take the drugs, and that I don't forget. I struggle with this, I mean how can I possibly fail? He's put it on a plate, follow the guide and take the medicine. A bit like the Clarets after the defeat at the weekend. Just got to take the medicine. No point worrying about it. I'm not going to over-think it. Good old Sean, he's a line for every moment.

Lisa works away with the last two syringes and then asks that I hang around for a few minutes to check I'm not reacting badly. Quite what that bad reaction would entail I don't know; is she meaning check my temperature again and ask whether I'm feeling sick or nauseous? Or is there a risk that this is going to turn me into a fucking werewolf?

Eventually, by around 4pm, I am free to leave. I've been in the same room since 8.30am. And in the same chair for most of it. Quite restricted. It's been a plane journey in many ways. I could have got to New York in that time. Next session (should I start calling it sesh?) is 28 April. I can't wait for it to come around. I just pray that we get promoted by then. That will show them. Cancer can't stop me getting promoted.

I pack up my bag with all the things I brought with me but didn't need. As I'm leaving I can't resist a trip to the gents. I'm delighted to see illuminous red streaming out into the pot. I need to share this moment. I'm not a Facebook man and it's possibly not the right type of material even if I was. I take a photo of the pot which has now turned to Tizer. My brother will appreciate this. He'll be wondering how I've got on. I won't get into any of that shit. I text him the photo with the words 'chemo piss'. He'll get the gist of it. It's been grand. Onwards we go. E-I E-I E-I O, up the Football League we go!!!!!!

Tuesday 1 April 2014

I wake up to a pounding of my head, and it takes me a moment to realise that this is a physical attack on me rather than a bad headache. From the cushioned feel of what is slamming into my temple and forehead it can only be Oscar jumping up and down on me. Pampers-clad arse first. Nothing changes. Even with cancer. That's the good thing about having kids too young to realise what's going on.

I come to. How do I feel? Okay actually. I can tell I've had something. But not too much. I've no headache. I don't feel sick. I feel something. But it's mild. It's like, say, having four pints. Of just like lager or something. Where the next morning you can feel that you've had a drink the night before, but it doesn't feel like it's a problem.

By 10.30am I feel nothing. Apart from feeling completely normal. They told me that if I'm going to feel ill it will be within the first couple of days. So far so good then.

Wednesday 2 April 2014

I feel exhausted today. Not weak. Just tired. Last night I just could not sleep. If I slept I woke up not long after.

Catherine has googled it and she's telling me it's normal and it's the steroids I've taken. I can live with normal.

I still don't feel sick. I'm starving though.

I was ready to be feeling shit. It isn't happening the way it's meant to. It's not what I was expecting. Which is a good thing. Expect the unexpected. It happens all the time in football. Matches, seasons, players – it doesn't always turn out the way the bookie thinks it will.

Like Chris Waddle and Glen Little in 1997/98: at the beginning of the season I was delighted with the appointment of Waddle – everybody was – and the bookmakers had us as favourites for promotion. I had barely heard of Glen Little – he was a squad player who never got a game.

It didn't happen that way. Instead, Burnley flirted outrageously with relegation in 1997/98 under Chris Waddle. It was a shame, I was a massive Waddle fan, but once he'd finished with us I wasn't! He'd probably not played enough football below the top division, and underestimated it. He filled the squad with has-beens and young players rejected by Premier League clubs who weren't up to it. Ultimately, we stayed up by the skin of our teeth, and whilst we celebrated the last-ditch win over Plymouth on the final day of the season, we weren't really celebrating, not the next day anyway. Something great came out of that season though. We came to realise that we had one of the most talented players outside the Premier League at the club, and he would be the catalyst for the success that we had over the next few seasons. His name was Glen Little.

We'd signed him from Glentoran in November 1996 and he'd rarely played. It was a home match against Brentford where I became convinced we'd been hiding a world-beater, who, according to our assistant manager at the time Glen Roeder, 'wasn't fit to lace Waddle's boots'. Big, awkward, with a gangly frame, he would run at the opposition with the ball, try to take them on, have success in doing so, and put crosses in. He also did the other bits; he got back, put tackles in, and actually looked like he gave a shit. Burnley fans love somebody who tracks back and tackles and looks like they want it.

They call it trying. I call it visually trying. It buys you a load of time and goodwill with supporters. If on top of that you're a proper player and do that old-fashioned thing called dribbling then they'll love you forever. I fell for Glen Little that day. And I told him so after the game.

I was only 16 but I'd started going out in Burnley town centre a while back, especially on a Saturday night. We were in Paradise Island (couldn't be much further from paradise but I see what they were aiming for) and there he was, with another of our players, Paul Weller. I was drunk but not hammered and had no hesitation in approaching Glen and telling him how well I thought he'd played and that the Burnley fans were going to love him for his ability and his attitude. To his credit he didn't dismiss the kid in front of him but chatted to me for a good 20 minutes about the match, the club, the fans, and his hopes.

Glen Little is a Burnley legend. Top man. And, contrary to what Roeder thought, in 1998 he was more than fit to lace Chris Waddle's boots. And, by the way, I'm starving, not feeling sick. There's no hurricane yet.

Thursday 4 April 2014

I'm getting a funny sensation in my neck where my tumour is. I can't describe it. Not a tingling. More a fizzing feel. It's that Tizer on a treasure hunt. I touch my neck. I check the mirror. Is this magic juice working? Already? I think it is.

I ask the wife for a second opinion.

'Michael, no, don't do this … you're just trying to tell yourself that. I don't want you to be disappointed.'

Maybe she's right. I feel high. I can't work it out. I feel so pumped up for this I can't tell whether I'm being optimistic, positive, or simply delusional.

So many people have asked me questions about statistics and chances of success (which means chances of survival, like to stay alive and not be dead, how are we even talking about this?) that I have to have an answer. The problem is I can't find anything detailed enough. I can find stats for non-Hodgkin lymphoma, I can find stats on Diffuse Large B Cell, stats on Stages, stats on age and so on, and sometimes these stats include more than one variable. But not all together. So I've found some stats on non-Hodgkin lymphoma Stage 1, and then made some 'manual adjustments' for sub type and age. I also figure that stats are based on history and generally the present and the future are better at curing stuff than the past so I make another manual adjustment for that. It's a bit like inflation. Plus I'm a drinker, I get points for that. And, most importantly, I'm from Burnley and I don't give a fuck. Eventually, when you crunch the numbers you come out with 99.99 per cent survival chance. I call it 'close to 100 per cent' when I'm asked.

Friday 5 April 2014

It's the weekend so that means it's time for a beer. I'm not going to let a bit of the old chemo ruin that for me. I'm doing it differently though. For the first time in my adult life I'm going to control or limit what I drink.

I have decided to go with Dr Ong's recommendation of 14 units per week. I'm going to take Sunday to Thursday off completely, and use up my 14 across Friday and Saturday, seven units each night. I figure if I can have say four 330ml bottles on each night that will put me on about 14 units, or maybe just under even. Spirits are out. Wine – which I don't drink unless you put it in front of me and then I do – is also out.

The problem with 330ml bottles of lager is that you get through the guts of one on your first swig. Now then, swig, what a word. 'Give us a swig of that,' Jesus, would you even share a drink with somebody who has asked for a swig? This is fine when you have no limits and an endless supply until you pass out, but when you're rationed to four, you don't need to drain one, i.e. a quarter of your ration, before you've even started.

I reflect on this mistake. I think I've started drinking not just with beer thirst, but also an element of natural thirst. That's contributed to this situation. Going forward, I can make use of other drinks to quench this natural thirst. You know, stuff like water and that. I've not thought of this before, but using alcohol as a thirst quencher is a bit nuts. I do it though. I need to drink more water. Lions drink water. Too bad I'm not a lion.

Saturday 5 April 2014
Watford v Burnley

We go out for breakfast with the kids. I haven't felt this fresh on a Saturday morning in years. And I need to. Eating out with these two maniacs is essentially a sport. Some people spend their weekends in the gym. I go to Frankie & Benny's and bend down under the table (head right down past my knees so I feel sick), picking up little men off the floor, keeping my wits about me to react cat-like to catch anything being indiscriminately tossed off the table (crockery and glassware), and then doing relays back and forth to the toilets just for fun. If we're in a really good mood we might also do a circuit chase around the restaurant for five minutes on the way out.

As we're sat there I feel the Tizer in my neck again. I touch it. Yeah this is smaller, it's this tingling it really is, and I know I'm not wrong.

'Is it smaller?' I ask Catherine.

She looks at me. She looks concerned. Then puzzled. A smile breaks from the corner of her lips.

'It is,' she moves to touch it.

'Yes it is, it's definitely smaller.'

She's touching it more.

'Yes, that is way smaller.'

Affirmation.

I'm not wrong, am I? I'm not delusional. This Tizer juice is at it right now as we're sat here in Frankie & Benny's. Fizzing the fuck out of the cancer in my neck. On a treasure hunt. Get in! It feels good. I'm climbing finally. Three points to take me out of the relegation zone.

Burnley are away this afternoon at Vicarage Road against Watford. I've been there a couple of times; once not long ago, the 2004 FA Cup quarter-final. I say not long ago, it's been ten years. These years fly by at the moment. What I have achieved in that time. Not a great deal. I've got married, had a kid, got divorced, moved country, moved jobs, moved jobs back but not country, got married, had two more kids.

Well that afternoon in 2004 was pure shite. Burnley just didn't turn up and limped to a 2-0 defeat.

My 1995 visit was just as bad. This was our one-off season in the Championship/Division One which ended up in relegation. We got hammered 3-0 and we got soaked wet through in the rain. It was a great day though. It was a Burnley Boys' Club day out, first for a tour of Wembley Stadium in the morning, followed by the Burnley match in the afternoon. We must have left the house at 5am to drive up Colne Road to get the coach. I felt sick. It's an unnatural hour to be awake at. We stopped off at a newsagent's in Coal Clough Lane for a paper – it was open. Why?

The tour of Wembley was good anyway. Complete dump it was but a good one. It's hard to believe now how the FA let Wembley get into such a state, but in 1995 it was an absolute dump. The TV studio, though, was superb. Sky TV had been there in the week I think for an England game. The desk the presenters sat at was clean, the floor beneath it littered with empty beer cans. It looked like a nightclub on a Sunday morning. I was amazed by this. Those fellas on TV, they drink beer whilst working. Walking around the perimeter of the pitch, down the players' tunnel, that massive vast tunnel, was amazing. One of my favourite photographs was taken there – me with my grandad who was twice the size of me, and Wembley in the background.

The match, though, wasn't great. The promotion the season before had been a lucky one and we weren't really ready for that division. We couldn't handle it. But what were the strange accents? I'd been to loads of Burnley away games but not so much in London. It was the first time I heard London accents in the Burnley end. But these weren't Watford fans, they were Burnley fans. And there were a good few of them. I learnt a lesson – Burnley fans are everywhere.

For today's game we are struggling with injuries. Ingsy being out was bad enough, but now we're missing Vokesy as well. You wonder if we have enough goals in us. Again, I'm following the game on Sky Sports News. We go 1-0 down early on to a Troy Deeney goal. Please, please, please do not get beat. Not after last weekend – we need to get back on track. I pace around the room watching the ticker at the bottom of the screen, hoping, praying, that the next goal flashing up is a Burnley one. Getting a result today (any kind of points) will be just brilliant, it will prove that we've got the mental robustness. When I can handle it no longer I leave the room and throw a few darts. Get rid of some of the tension. I play a game with myself. I won't go back in to check the score until I've thrown a treble 20. Then when I do go back in, we'll have scored, maybe. And I'll have made it happen, maybe. It's got to be better than pacing the room anyway.

It takes me about ten minutes and over 100 throws but eventually one nestles in the 60 box. Right, now, let's go check, please have scored, please, please, please.

I walk towards the TV, and as I get nearer I slowly make out the text at the bottom of the ticker. It somehow takes me ages to work out the shape of the name of the player who's scored and the scoreline and team names next to it. Then I see it – Arfield – 87 – Watford 1 – 1 Burnley.

We've scored!! Get in!!! It finishes one apiece. It's a point. But a great one. After last week's defeat we didn't want another. We're back in the saddle.

Sunday 6 April 2014

I've still got my hair, which is what they said would be the case at this stage. But nobody told me about the black tongue. It looks like I've gone mental on Black Jacks. A quick google reveals it is indeed a common, harmless side effect of chemo. It's basically dead cells on your tongue nuked by the chemo. It's brushed off with a toothbrush easy enough. It just looks a bit weird. But, if you've eaten plenty of Black

Jacks as a kid, and at 1p each I occasionally bought 50 (plus 50 Fruit Salads, which I always kind of regarded as Black Jacks' sister sweet), you won't be disturbed by black tongue.

Monday 7 April 2014

Tizer. Tizer, you magical treasure hunting fizz. My eyes don't deceive me. My fingers and thumbs don't either. There is nothing to see. There is nothing to feel. Tumour. My source of paranoia. My chip on my shoulder (neck). My elephant man feature. My massive overgrown neck bollock. You are dead, you big fat fuck.

The fizzing has continued. It's not that frequent. Maybe once or twice a day for a few seconds only. But when I rub my fingers across my neck now all I feel is a ridge along the line of my biopsy incision. I can't tell whether it's tumour or scar. If in doubt take the positive answer. Scar it is.

Actually, though, let's think about this. This was bound to happen. It was bloody obvious, wasn't it? Why? Because the truth is that I don't have cancer after all. It's a mistake. All these doctors have missed it. I've got something that looks a bit like cancer, but it isn't. It's a new thing that nobody has had before. Pretty harmless but unexplainable. We'll have to give it a name – perhaps 'Heinicke mild' – sounds like a beer from the 1970s – Hodgkin will be well annoyed. Anyway, whatever we call it, one chemo has killed it so job done.

I phone Dr Ong. This is going to be very embarrassing for her. But hey, it's a misdiagnosis. It must happen occasionally. And I'm not bothered. I'm just glad that it's done. I won't sue them. It's fine.

'Are you okay, Mr Heinicke?'

'Yes, I'm grand. It's gone.'

'What do you mean?'

'The tumour, it's completely gone.'

'Already?'

'Yes.'

'Well that's good.'

'Would that normally happen? With this?'

'Well, it would be unusual for it to work so quickly but not a bad thing, it's good.'

'So, do you think we still need to treat this?'

'Yes Mr Heinicke, you need to have six cycles of RCHOP.'

'Even though it's gone?'

'Mr Heinicke, you are very sick ...'

'No I'm not sick.'

I hate this word sick. I'm not. I have a predisposition which if left untreated will increase the chances of me being sick. But I'm not sick. Not yet anyway.

'Mr Heinicke, you have non-Hodgkin lymphoma. You need six cycles of RCHOP.'

'Well before you were saying maybe three maybe six, could we not just do the three then?'

'Mr Heinicke, the multidisciplinary team have agreed that you need six cycles.'

Well that wasn't how I'd planned it. So it looks like I definitely have this cancer. Hmmm. Well that's not too bad. That's what I thought. Until about an hour ago when I went off on one. It's as you were.

The advice is that I shouldn't travel on a plane or be in large crowds in public. The reason for this is that I have low immunity and am more likely to pick up an infection in a crowd. But there's no way I'm missing nanna's funeral tomorrow. I take the Flybe plane from City Airport to Manchester and this time manage not to cry.

I watch George at his football training session in the evening. He's no idea there's anything wrong with me and long may it stay that way. I'm glad he's getting into football at the moment. I shouldn't care but for a year or two I thought he was never going to be interested. He's only seven, I really shouldn't worry. It's not that I want him to be into football so that he can be a footballer and all that and earn loads of money. I want him to be into football because if he isn't I'm worried he'll miss out. Plus, what the hell will I talk to him about if he's not? This season and Burnley's superb performance is probably helping him. Well done again Sean.

In August 1988 when I'd just gone seven, so slightly younger than George is now, me and our Jim did a five-day residential course at Bobby Charlton's Soccer School in Manchester. David Beckham was probably there. I don't know why there aren't any pictures of me with Bobby Charlton.

There could well be though. Charlton was massively hands-on. I thought absolutely nothing of it at the time, but it just wouldn't happen like that anymore. There was only about seven or eight groups of kids and each group only had around 20 or so, maybe less. I'd imagine the modern equivalent has about 4,000 kids, like a conveyor belt.

Charlton was there every day. He sat down and ate lunch with the kids, most of the time at my table with the youngest age group. He got out on the training pitch too, going from group to group. He was watching my group one day when we were playing 'king of the ring'. It's a 20 by 20 grid, each kid has a ball, and the aim is to keep control of your own ball whilst trying to kick out everybody else's. If your ball goes outside the grid you're out. The last player left is king of the ring. So we were doing this and I got down to the last two players. Anyone who's played this knows what can happen – you both get too cautious of guarding your own ball and there can be a bit of a stand-off. This happened for all of about ten seconds then into the ring stepped Bobby to settle it. Me and the other lad looked at each other, looked at Bobby, what was he going to do? I had a 50:50 chance of winning this depending on which way he went. Bobby came straight for me, nicked my ball off my toe, and booted it out of the square. Cheers Bobby, thanks.

It was a brilliant week, all football related. The nights were light so we'd have kickabouts on the grass without any coaches or supervision of any description. There was a Subbuteo shop that sold random Subbuteo stuff really cheap (presumably because they couldn't flog it at full price) so we came home with loads of random Scottish teams. And we played loads of football. I managed an overhead kick in a proper game context. I didn't score but the coaches singled me out for praise for the effort.

I saw a condom for the first time, too. The Soccer School was based at Manchester Met, using the halls of residence, dining rooms and football pitches. Walking back from the pitches one day, a few older lads were throwing what looked like a deflated balloon at each other, but someone pointed out that this was in fact a 'rubber jonny'. I didn't question it, even though I was secretly wondering who jonny was.

Best of all was my nickname for the week. My group had more than one Michael, as you would find amongst 20 boys in the 1980s. But there was only one Burnley fan, it was the first time the boys in my group had met one, and the first time they'd met anyone wearing a Burnley shirt. My name that week … Burnley. It's a great name, I gave it to my cat when I was 26.

It felt as though the doctors didn't quite know where they were at. Six or three is a big difference. Double. But actually more than double. Before I start any treatment I can see it as a football season. The first one, potentially two, are early season optimism. Shiny new kits. There is a novelty to it.

Even with cancer there is a novelty. There is. Human nature. The weather is nicer too. The last one you're on the home straight at the end of the season. Provided you're not being relegated (so, dying would be my equivalent here) you're happy, looking forward to next season – maybe a promotion, or a hope of one next year.

The tricky bit comes in the middle – October to March – worse in December/January/ February – the mid-season slogging it out in mud.

This is where three versus six is a big deal. With three rounds of chemo my middle slog is one chemo, tops. With six rounds my mid-season is as many as four. So it's four times as bad. I would have preferred three.

Catherine wanted three.

I hadn't realised – I didn't google enough – three rounds of RCHOP is the norm for Stage 1 non-Hodgkin lymphoma Diffuse Large B-Cell. Which is what I have. Six rounds is normal for Stage Two. I'm not Stage Two, am I? I don't think so. Catherine is panicked by this. I don't know whether she thinks I'm lying about my staging. But it seems that they are treating me like a Stage Two.

I asked Dr Alshoufi about it and he said it was because the tumour was 'massive'.

Catherine has done some googling and she has read that Stage One Bulky might get the same as Stage Two. Bulky, now there's a word.

Tuesday 8 April 2014

Big day all round. It's my nanna's funeral this morning. And tonight Burnley have a big game away at Barnsley.

My brother has flown home from Cayman so it's good to catch up with him. The only problem I can see is that me and our Jim don't do well together in church. We find everything highly amusing and giggle like teenage girls high on alcopops. We've always done this. Since we were five and seven. Alcopops hadn't even been invented then.

We're waiting in the reception area of the funeral home. It's just me and our Jim. My mum and dad are somewhere in the building with the funeral people. My nanna was divorced before I was even born.

In the days when nobody got divorced. She was a pioneer. Ahead of her time. She remarried (to Terry) nearly 20 years ago. His health isn't great either. Physically he's doing okay, but he has Alzheimer's or dementia or something like that and is clearly losing his marbles. It wasn't that clear before my nanna got sick but the lid on that has now been lifted. My uncle Tony has gone to collect him.

'Mick, look.'

I move to where our Jim is standing and follow his eyes out of the window to the car park.

'What the fuck is he wearing?'

I try my best but I can't hold it in. I burst into a fit of laughter. We're not even in church yet. Tony is helping Terry to the building. Terry is wearing a very light suit. Light grey. But very light. Not that far off white. I've no idea why he owns such an item. I'm absolutely clueless as to why he's wearing it to his wife's funeral. If I didn't know better I would think he's intentionally trying to disrespect her.

As they enter the building, Tony shakes hands with a couple of the funeral home staff. Terry follows suit. But then he moves to me and our Jim. And shakes our hands too. Bloody hell, he thinks we work here. He's no idea who we are.

My mum appears.

'Anthony ... where is his suit?'

'Terry, where's your suit?'

Tony looks flustered. Terry is grinning like a Cheshire cat but he's no idea why. He doesn't even know what day it is.

'Couldn't find it.'

'Anthony … at 8 o'clock last night I left it hung up in his bedroom.'

'Well … he's lost it.'

You can say that again.

Afterwards we're in the Rosegrove Unity Working Men's Club. This was actually my grandad's club, my nanna had no connection to it, but it's the nearest place to the cemetery where we've just buried her.

The majority of the people here know me, and most of them haven't seen me since I got diagnosed. I look completely normal. The tumour has gone now, my hair is still intact. I'm having a few pints at my nanna's funeral. You couldn't pick me out in a line-up as the cancer victim.

A middle-aged family friend who I've known all my life but not seen for a year or two hugs me, and, for the first time ever, tells me that she loves me. I'm assuming this is because I have cancer. It's crackers.

Another middle-aged chap and his wife tell me how great I'm looking. I don't know what to say. Thanks, I guess. But I'm thinking, I've only just started here, we haven't got to the disco yet. I've barely even got my dancing shoes on. Another person joins them, and another, and now there's four people circling me telling me how great I look. 'Fantastic,' one of them says. Again, I've never experienced this before, you would think I was a fucking catwalk model the amount of compliments I'm getting on my appearance.

Focus has quickly moved to the Burnley game tonight. We're away at Barnsley. Every male here seems to be going – at least the ones I'm talking to are. I'd love to be going. But a night match with a big crowd isn't good for my immunity according to Dr Ong, who is effectively my new boss. We could really do with a win tonight – we haven't won in the last two games – not a bad run – but if you want to get automatic promotion out of the Championship you can't have a bad run.

The last time we got promoted in 2008/09, incredibly we had a run of five consecutive defeats around Christmas. Actually, that included a defeat at Barnsley. How we got promoted that season I've no idea. It was via the play-offs for a start, we were nowhere near an automatic spot. We got fifth place and played teams who were on downers for not having got automatic (because they had different expectations). We had enough luck and romance about us to get through. We were lucky though.

I'm a big fan of things starting badly and then getting better. I love a good comeback. Last-minute winner. Phoenix from the ashes. Up against it. The day of the long odds.

2008/09 was just that.

We started shockingly with defeats away at Wednesday and home to Ipswich. Next up was a trip to Crystal Palace.

Our Jim was about to emigrate to the Caribbean around this time so a stag do-style away day was appropriate. It was the back end of August, and even though we'd started badly, it was early enough for us to still have plenty of new season optimism in us as we drank in the sun outside The George pub off Borough High Street near London Bridge.

That optimism had evaporated by the time we got to a pub in Croydon after the match.

Burnley had been below bad. The game had finished 0-0, which we'd have taken before the game. But Palace had been down to nine men for a lot of it, and we'd still not even troubled them. We'd only scored one goal in the first two games and conceded seven. We now had a point on the board at least, but if we can't score or even look like scoring against nine men, well, we're in trouble.

Chatting to a Palace fan in the pub afterwards, I shared my new found pessimism

'Carry on like that,' I told him, 'and I think we're going down.'

'Yeah, based on today, I think you are,' he replied.

Sometimes it's nice to be wrong. That was a time. Nice to be surprised.

This season it's different. We're second in the league. And we deserve to be. It feels more earnt. This is the difference between Sean Dyche and Owen Coyle. Coyle was bluffing, all the time, he talked shite and we believed it, but there was no real substance, just luck and romance. Dyche, though, he's the real deal. No bullshit, pure honesty. But ultra-positive. It's brilliant. We have to deal with reality. But let's have the positive thoughts.

I'm home in Bangor by the time the game starts. We score early through Ashley Barnes to put us into a one-nil lead and it's the only goal of the game. Get in Burnley.

Thursday 10 April 2014

For a couple of days now I've been waking up with hairs in my mouth. They're my hairs – from my head. Not many, just a few. But it only takes one hair in your mouth to feel like you're choking. There's a few hairs on my pillow too. It's happening. Right on cue. I'm surprised on a couple of counts. Despite them telling me that it would, I was convinced it wouldn't happen to me. I'm in a different club to the rest of them. I mean, my tumour vanished in a few days. I thought my body would resist. Apparently not. So fair enough it's falling out, but I thought it would be faster once it had started, not just a few hairs at a time. At this rate it will take months for it to fall out. Except that I've got kids, though, and obviously an element of any week involves them pulling my hair. Not for any reason, just for a laugh. So when Sam pulls on my hair and realises that he has taken a handful with him, he wonders what is going on. He's only three – he doesn't know anything about cancer, chemotherapy. He doesn't even know I'm sick.

Yes, I've conceded that we can use that word to describe my state. I'm fed up of arguing about it. As long as you don't tell me I have a disease. He stares at me and grins. This is quite funny I think. I invite him to have another go. He takes another generous helping. He can't quite understand what's going on but can't get any words out, just hysterical laughter. I'm laughing too. It's definitely not falling out the way they said it would at the open day. I wonder if this is standard practice. Or maybe it is, but only in madhouses such as this one?

After a few minutes of hair-pulling fun I decide I need to assess the damage, but he doesn't want the game to end. 'Last one?' he asks reaching for me again, as though he's asking for another go on the slide as we try to extract him from a play park.

I oblige one final time and then check the mirror. Yep, he's completely butchered it. Time to shave it off. I grab my hair clippers, put the number-one attachment on, and get rid of it.

Friday 11 April 2014

The next chemo is going to be different. I'm going to have no hair. I'm going to wear shorts. And hopefully it will be much faster.

And I want to be Premier League by then. Not that any of the nurses have a clue, or that there is any point in telling

May 1988 – me (right) and Jim – ready for Wembley and the Sherpa Van Trophy Final v Wolves.

July 1988 – Majorca – with my mum and dad – me modelling some 'merchandise' from the club shop

Panini Football 87 – Kevin Gage – why the fuck did I put you in twice?

October 1989 – me being cool in a 1989 way

1991 – Christ the King RC Primary football team – that's me ruining the balance of the photograph by insisting I have the ball

1992 – Jimmy Mullen's Claret and Blue Army – I still have it 26 years later

June 1992 – my hair needed a comb; hers just needed shears

April 1992 – Burnley schools cup final – St Teds (blue) v Barden – I'm third from the left back row, between two keepers. Must have been taken before the game because we hammered them

August 1993 – Burnley Boys Club under 13s – I'm front row, second left – our manager, Eric (great bloke) seems to be wearing a Glasgow Rangers goalkeeper's shirt

June 1994 – AC Inter winning a trophy (or perhaps a windmill) – I won more trophies than I made appearances with that team

February 1995 – Wembley – with my grandad – before Burnley's defeat to Watford at Vicarage Road

BLACKBURN ROVERS FOOTBALL AND ATHLETIC PLC

Registered Office: EWOOD PARK, BLACKBURN, LANCS. BB2 4JF
Telephone: 0254 698888 · Fax: 0254 671042

Our Ref: AI/KAB

16th May 1994

Mr & Mrs Heinicke
3 Howarth Close
Burnley

Dear Mr & Mrs Heinicke

I am writing to thank you and Michael for your effort and committment to the Centre Of Excellence this season.

I have taken this opportunity to enclose a Centre Of Excellence registration form for next season which must be completed and returned to me, together with two passport photographs by the 1st June 1994. Please read this form carefully and ensure that you sign it on the back. A specimen form is enclosed to assist you in completing the new form.

Coaching sessions for next season will not commence until August and I will write to you further with full details nearer the time.

Yours sincerely
BLACKBURN ROVERS FOOTBALL & ATHLETIC PLC

ALAN IRVINE
YOUTH TEAM COACH

1994 – letters from Alan Irvine – a top coach and my favourite ever Bastard

BLACKBURN ROVERS FOOTBALL AND ATHLETIC PLC

Registered Office: EWOOD PARK, BLACKBURN, LANCS. BB2 4JF
Telephone: 0254 698888 · Fax: 0254 671042

Our Ref: AI/KAB

26th August 1994

Mr & Mrs Heinicke
2 Howorth Close
BURNLEY
Lancs
BB11 2RA

Dear Mr & Mrs Heinicke

I refer to my previous letter and would advise that coaching sessions will commence at the Blackburn Rovers Indoor Centre (B.R.I.C.), on Tuesday 6th September 1994. The sessions will be on Tuesday's and Thursday's from 7.45 pm to 9.00 pm.

Michael should report to the Dressing Rooms at the B.R.I.C. at 7.35 pm wearing kit suitable for training on an indoor astroturf pitch.

The B.R.I.C. is situated about 100 yards from the Darwen End of Ewood Park. If you require directions please contact me or Jim Furnell at the ground.

I look forward to meeting you on the 6th September.

Yours sincerely
BLACKBURN ROVERS FOOTBALL & ATHLETIC PLC

ALAN IRVINE
YOUTH TEAM COACH

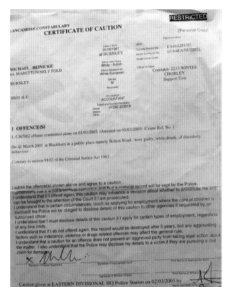

March 2005 – another Blackburn related letter…

May 2009 – Wembley – just before the Championship play-off victory over Sheffield United – the shorts were a mistake – the Kronenbourg wasn't

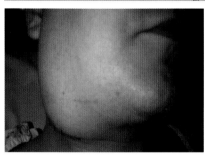

7 March 2014 – post biopsy selfies – neck stitched back together with a primary school stapler

31 March 2014 – just before chemo 1 – massive bollock on my neck

31 March 2014 – chemo live! Drinking Colombian coffee and practising texting

4 April 2014 – fizzing away to fuck – and me doing my Phil Neville impression

13 April 2014 – the only bollocks on my neck now are Oscar's

8 May 2014 – hopefully this is what I might look like when I'm 62, not 32

June and July 2014 – having cancer didn't change the fact that Oscar wanted to live on my shoulders

2 September 2014 – Ulster Hospital – Sam and Oscar trying out Brian's bed

19 September 2014 – Majorca – hoping that Sam doesn't miss from there

October 2014 – Clandeboye Park, Bangor – me (in red jacket) with my Ards 2007 squad

April 2015 – with my new curly hair. That's Sam next to me, and Oscar on my shoulders again

30 April 2016 – promotion day for Ards FC at Clandeboye Park. Sam doing something weird with his cheeks on the off chance that the photo would end up in a book

July 2016 – Lanzarote – me, Sam, Finn and Oscar

*Christmas Day 2015 –
Catherine with six-week-
old Finn*

*22 October 2016 –
Blacko, Lancashire
– before Sam's first
Burnley game, a 2-1
win over Everton*

*4 November 2017 – Ards v
Crusaders – George and former
Burnley keeper Brian Jensen
(aka 'Beast')*

2017 – Majorca – with Finn – I hate beaches but I love football pitches

December 2018 – Sam with Dyche before the 2-0 win over West Ham

2018 – Finn 'hiding' from Sam and Oscar

them about it, or that it makes any difference. Next time I step foot in the McDermott Unit I want to be Premier League. I just do. It's a target I've set myself. The fact I can't actually influence it at all is irrelevant. I need targets and aspirations. It's hanging over me, just like this cancer. I know I can't sort the cancer out by then, but if I could at least get this promotion over the line and boxed off, well, that would be good. That would be something.

My hair isn't right. Once I shaved it off I could see that there are parts of my head that are completely bald – right down to the skin. I couldn't see this before. These bald patches are maybe only the size of a 2p coin but there are lots of them scattered over my head. Then the rest of it is number-one length. It makes me look like a zebra. I take the clippers out again and bring it all to the bone. It's all shiny now. It looks better. Still, it does make me look a bit cancer.

Saturday 12 April 2014
Burnley v Boro

Boro are another of those clubs who were on a different level to us when I was growing up. They spent a lot of years in the First Division/Premier League when we were nowhere near, the exception being the 1994/95 season when we were both in the second tier. They were still miles ahead of us then – they had Bryan Robson as manager, a new stadium, and fancy Italian kits. They got promoted and we got relegated to restore what at the time was parity.

But now we're equal, in fact we're above them, so this is a game we should win.

We don't though. We get beat 1-0.

It ruins my weekend, a defeat like this. We've got beat. I've got cancer. What's happening? I need the next game and

I need it now. Get back on track. We need to put this right. I need Sean to calm me down. I know he will.

Another healthy gate at Turf Moor though, over 18,000. That's more than twice as many as we were getting in the late 1980s when I started going.

Prior to the modernisation in 1996 the Cricket Field Stand at Turf Moor was a home end. We gave the away fans about a third of the Longside terrace, and, as far as I can remember, no seats anywhere in the ground.

It holds around 4,000 and back in the late 1980s and early 1990s it was typically half full, with most fans sitting towards the middle and rear of the stand. The gradient of the Cricket Field is a lot shallower than the rest of the stands at the Turf, and the gangways a lot wider. Back in the 1980s, it was a stand where a kid could do a lot of running about – there was space to roam and it was safe. Two of the lads from my primary school class, Woody and Stanny, were also season-ticket holders, so every home game we would meet up inside the stand and go off on our own somewhere. We'd take in multiple seats each game, and in turn we'd get a complete passive smoking experience, taking in a variety of different tobacco products. I've never been a smoker but even now when I'm around tobacco smoke I reminisce about the Cricket Field End.

Up until recently, Turf Moor was the only stadium in the Football League to have the players' tunnel located in the stand behind the goal (Blackpool also had one but theirs disappeared a few years earlier). We'd hang over the edge of the white brick tunnel four times each game – kick-off, once either side of half-time and the full-time whistle. In those days there wasn't an extendable tunnel that the players could hide behind. The tunnel was properly exposed into the stand so you could give the away team plenty of shit.

We'd also, on occasion, take a seat in the block of the stand in the bottom left as you look at the pitch. That was the corner nearest to the away section of the Longside. The three of us would sit there, the only people in the block, and do our best to goad the away fans. Nothing ever happened. We were under ten years old for most of this period of time, we didn't look threatening, we weren't loud, and they probably didn't even notice us. We fully believed that if we started singing 'Who the fucking hell are you?' or, dare I say it, 'Come and have a go if you think you're hard enough?' that nobody actually cared. Until Darlington came to town in about 1990.

Like most teams in the basement division, their away following was pitiful and barely made a dent on the vast expanse of terracing they'd been given. From the Cricket Field Stand you could see clearly enough to count the visiting supporters on the Longside – the lowest I saw was six Hereford fans at a night match in the early 1990s – Darlington that day had brought about 100. The fewer fans there are, the easier it is to spot erratic movements, and whilst we were in full song I did see a few of them darting about the terrace. The movements looked out of place. We were still singing as a couple of them ran towards us and started climbing the fence to get out of the Longside and into the Cricket Field End, right in the corner where we were sitting. I can still see the lad at the front now, thin, wiry type, about 20 and wearing glasses. Glasses? Is he taking the piss?

We've started a riot, I thought. 'Quick, get help,' shouted Woody, as the three of us stopped our singing and clambered up the seats behind us. We knew where all the big men sat, the ones who would not stand for this, and as we ran up the steps we saw our saviours running down towards us. Big solid lads, built like brick shithouses, about 20 of them.

'Darlington down there,' we told them, and pointed to the area of the stand from where we'd retreated.

It felt like a close encounter. We had started a riot. Me, Woody and Stanny.

It took a few years for it to dawn on me that we hadn't incited the trouble that day. Those Darlington fans had turned up looking for it and tried to find it on both sides of their terrace. Like all the other teams, they didn't give a damn what three kids were singing and they probably couldn't even hear our wee voices. But I didn't know that at the time. I was scared and grateful to see those stand boys running down the steps ready for battle. And even as an eight-year-old I was proud. Proud that we had supporters who weren't prepared to take any shit.

Monday 14 April 2014

The bastard mouthwash.

Bloody hell. When they gave me the bag of take home medicine I sort of ignored the mouthwash. After all, there were steroids in there, loads of other pills, and a bottle of laxative (which, let's face it, always makes one chuckle a bit). So the mouthwash, I didn't really think much about. The idea is that mouth ulcers/sores are a common way to get an infection and so using this mouthwash twice daily minimises the chances of mouth ulcers/sores, and hence getting an infection. Makes sense.

Well, if I was expecting a green or blue 'minty fresh' type by Colgate or similar I could think again. This is dark red industrial stuff, basically petrol, which tastes a bit like aftershave. Swirl it round your mouth for 30 seconds. Spit it out. And then drink a gallon of water to get rid of the burning.

In the morning it's not too bad, although you can forget about actually being able to taste any breakfast. Luckily, I've never been much of a breakfast fan. 'Breakfast is for wimps,' as Del Boy once said. I used to quote that to my mum when I was eating a KitKat instead of cereal.

At night it's a mare – you either wake up with a burnt-out mouth needing a hose pipe down your throat, or alternatively you've had enough water to quell the mouth flames but wake up needing to piss.

It's funny the discipline you get into. I'm now officially a twice-a-day tooth brusher. I mean like every day without fail. It's always something I'd aspired to, but because of the drinking (i.e. drink – drink – drink – comatose) there was never a time to fit in a second brush of the day. Not every day anyway. I've also started doing a bit of the old flossing. I'm like the all-American kid. Except for my wonky teeth that is.

Oh yeah, and the stains. Another side effect of the mouthwash. Within a few days of using it I started to get brown marks on my teeth, like the coffee-coloured ones that you sometimes see on the teeth of people aged 60 plus and you wonder how the fuck they let them get like that. They look particularly bad in an old tart when set off against bright red lipstick. You know, the types drinking in Wetherspoon's at 2pm on a Tuesday, with their shopping trolleys. Yeah, so, I've started getting these marks, and despite vigorous brushing they can't be shifted. It's not a great look. I'm bald. And I look like I've eaten a bowl of shit. And I'm still overweight (clinically, I'm obese, but there are plenty of fat lads about).

Tuesday 15 April 2014

I can't wait for Friday. It's Good Friday which means there is a full programme of fixtures. Burnley have a local derby away at Blackpool.

The problem with this cancer is that I'm bored. Not enough happens during the day. It wasn't so bad a few weeks back when I was doing all those hospital gigs. TV is crap and Sky Sports News is a bit repetitive when you've watched it for over an hour. Sometimes I watch Sky Sports News for three hours solid. I can recite the news stories with the presenter I've heard them that many times.

I decide to do a few jobs around the house. There is always stuff that needs doing. Problem is I prefer to do things that don't need doing but are more fun. So I decide to build a surround for my dart board.

The dart board has come in handy these last couple of months. I'm not that good though, and to be honest I'm not trying to be. It's more of therapy. Go in there, shut the door and throw for an hour. The walls don't look happy though – they are suffering like downtown Beirut in the 1980s.

I've decided to buy cork tiles and glue them on to the wall and then frame the tiles with a border which I'll make from that kind of skirting you use for laminate flooring. I could just leave it at that, but I've time on my hands, so that border needs finishing. It's a good job I live near Homebase because it takes me a good few testers to find the right shade of claret. It's not red, or dark red, or maroon or burgundy. It's claret. Even the club themselves have got it wrong on occasions. The 1991/92 Fourth Division championship kit was a good example of this. Looking at it now, it was awful. At the time I loved it. Made by Ribero, it was more like purple. To make it worse, it wasn't just purple, it was purple with sky blue flecks. The sleeves were blue with white flecks. The word 'fleck' probably underplays how hideous this shirt was. You could easily exchange 'fleck' for 'bird shit'. The shirt was released and went on sale pretty much on the day of the first home game of the season. There was no launch or build-up or lead time as such. It arrived in the shop and they started selling it. The shop wasn't a shop. It was a room with a counter. There was no stock on the public side of the counter. The one window was tiny, with a metal grille on it. The new shirt was in the window but you couldn't call it a window display. I instantly loved it. It was different. I bought it the first day.

But as far at the dart board surround border goes, I'm not having purple or bird shit. I eventually settle on a Dulux shade they call 'Cherry Red'. It's not red, it's claret. The blue I find much easier, although it ends up being a tiny bit too much Man City sky for my liking.

The completed job looks like Burnley between 1989 and 1991. We had a shirt produced by Ellgren.

By the 1990/91 season we were getting a bit bored of Division Four and fancied ourselves for promotion.

A home game against Gillingham sticks in the memory. It was the first and only time I was mascot for Burnley. There were three mascots; me, our Jim, and another lad we didn't know. My Uncle Dave had sorted it for us.

It was also the first time I got into the nerve centre of the Cricket Field Stand, underneath where it all happens, the changing rooms, the manager's office and the boot room. It was so cramped. It was beautiful. The boot room was on the pitch side so had a slanted roof on one side; supporters were literally on top of you. It felt like it hadn't been renovated since it had been constructed 20-odd years earlier. And it probably hadn't.

Me and our Jim, by that stage in P6 and P7 respectively, had that morning played a football tournament for our school team. It had gone well. It was only a qualifying round, albeit on a round robin format, and we had qualified with ease. The pitches we'd played on at Eastern Avenue were a bog, so even though I'd half-heartedly cleaned my boots, as I got changed in the tiny boot room at Turf Moor I put my dry socks into two soaked football boots. They were squelching. These were one pair days for all kids. We didn't have 3G pitches. It was either inside on a hard surface, outside on a hard surface like tarmac or outside on grass (mud).

Modern mascots don't get the same experience as we did. These days the players are too pre-occupied warming up to entertain the mascots. The goalkeepers are having some one-on-one with the goalkeeping coach. That day, the Burnley goalkeeper Chris Pearce's warm-up involved three kids, three footballs, and him in the goals, and all three of us smacking the ball at him. We weren't even trying to warm him up. Eight yards out, have that in the bottom corner Pearcey, pick it out.

The game itself ended up being an anti-climax – we went 2-0 up but got pegged back and it finished 2-2 – a bit like the 1990/91 season in general terms as we made the play-offs only to be dumped out by Torquay United.

Friday 18 April 2014

Burnley is a small place. It's one of the smallest towns in England with a club in the Football League. I spent all of my childhood watching Burnley play in the lower two divisions. Despite all that, I grew up with a superiority complex. I genuinely believed Burnley FC to be the greatest sporting institution on the planet. And in some ways I still do; there is certainly something about Burnley that is different.

Events at matches like Carlisle United in 1992 created that view for me. Before we even got to Brunton Park I sort of knew what to expect. The fixture had, before postponements over the winter months, been scheduled to be the last away match of the season. Even though that wasn't the case, the traditional end of season rule still applied – Burnley fans (a lot of them anyway) wore fancy dress. The other thing was the small matter of promotion – a win would take Burnley back to the third tier after seven years in the basement division.

It was an invasion. Burnley were given the regular away-end terracing behind the goal and half of the seats in a stand alongside the pitch. As it filled up, Burnley fans took over the paddock terracing beneath those seats, and half of the opposite terrace. It was reported later that there were 9,000 Burnley fans in the ground that day. A sea of claret and blue dotted with Pink Panthers, rabbits, Roman soldiers and a man with a lilo who had a swim on the centre spot before the game. He got away with it without any heavy-handed policing, such was the carnival atmosphere. There was the occasional flashpoint; I saw a Burnley fan in the terracing below me kicking a Carlisle fan in the head but I didn't think much of it and neither did anybody else.

We went 1-0 up in the first half but Carlisle equalised in the second period meaning we had to settle for a 1-1 draw. It wasn't quite enough for promotion. We needed just one more point, and three more points to win the league.

Even though we hadn't won, we had won. It felt like a win to me anyway. I didn't feel frustrated. I was jubilant at what I had witnessed. We occupied a town. That town, Carlisle, must be used to that by now you'd have thought. Reasonably peacefully as well, save for a few local residents in tears about the number of cars parked in their cul-de-sacs.

As we walked away from the ground I noticed cars, some parked on streets, some in driveways, had flyers stuck under the windscreen wipers. Probably someone promoting something or preaching religion. As it turned out it was kind of neither and kind of both.

137

It simply read:

'YOU HAVE BEEN VISITED BY JIMMY
MULLEN'S CLARET AND BLUE ARMY'

They had as well.

Blackpool away. Live on Sky. The squad is down to the bare bones. But we need this win. I need a word with God on this one. Come on lad, I've still got cancer. Sort me out. We've only won one in the last four, scoring only twice. Ings and Vokes have been magnificent this season, and having them both out injured is far from ideal.

Blackpool are in a mess. They followed us into the Premier League in 2009/10, but, like us, lasted just a season and came straight back down in 2010/11. Unlike Burnley, they're not eyeing a return. The club is in complete disarray and the relationship between the owners and the fans is toxic. Nothing like Burnley.

We played Blackpool a lot when I was younger but not much since we got into the Championship in 2000. It's a local derby – but nothing like playing Blackburn, probably on a par with Preston North End. I've been to Bloomfield Road a couple of times but not for years and years, in the late 80s, early 90s I'm guessing. It was a dump back then; in fact, I think the large open-end terrace might have even been condemned at the time. One of them might have been an FA Cup game.

My memories are few; we collected some pies from a shop in Accrington Road in Burnley – it was called Jarvis – it might even have only sold pies. We ate them on the terrace at Bloomfield Road along the side – they were meat and potato, heavy on potato, lacking in meat, and full of pepper. We definitely got beat, that's for sure. And there was crowd trouble after the game outside the ground – I didn't see anything but could hear it, and could see the police racing to respond.

Bloomfield Road has changed since then; it's an all-seater since they hurriedly built some new stands when they got promoted to the Premier League for that single season. But it's still a dump, largely because they did it on the cheap, with a playing surface to match.

Blackpool at the Turf is a different animal. Back in 1990/91 we were both chasing promotion and we played them in a night game in April 1991. Turf Moor at night has a special atmosphere but that night stood out, largely because there were over 18,000 in the ground. For a fourth-tier match that was simply unheard of. Credit to Blackpool as well, they played their part. Until then I'd look at the Longside and see a swarm of Clarets on the right-hand side with the other side of the fence sparsely populated. That night, though, Blackpool filled it, and both sides of the Longside were rocking. It was one of only a handful of times I witnessed that. That tangerine colour as well, I wouldn't want it, but it definitely adds something to an away end.

In a tense game, Roger Eli gave Burnley the lead mid-way through the second half before John Deary sealed a 2-0 win late on. Ultimately, though, it didn't matter, as both teams got to the play-offs but missed out on promotion, with Blackpool losing to Torquay in the final after the same team had knocked Burnley out in the semis. That was a night to forget. Not helped by some Bastards fans who arranged to have a light aircraft fly over the Turf at half-time carrying a banner with the words 'Staying down 4 ever. Love Rovers. Ha ha ha'. And you wonder why we call them Bastards. As the minutes ticked down and Torquay knew they were going through to Wembley, their fans (not many of them) were singing 'Always look on the bright side of life'. I now recognise this as a *Monty Python* song but didn't at the time and I did not understand the lyrics. These boys were Wembley-bound – so how could there be a side of life that isn't bright? Surely this is everything and if you're a Torquay fan tonight there is only one side and it's shining brightly.

Right, then let's beat these Donkey Lashers and get ourselves promoted. It's going to be difficult now to meet my target of getting promoted, but take care of business and win our games and you never know what might happen.

There probably aren't many goals in us at the moment. But if we get a goal and take the lead, I'm confident we can defend it. We've let few goals in all season.

Half-time comes and there's not much in it. We haven't really looked like scoring but neither have Blackpool. Four minutes into the second half, I'm dancing around the living room as Michael Kightly scores a belter from outside the box. As soon as it hits the back of the net you can guess the final score. We won't risk looking for another. We'll defend this for a one-nil. That's exactly what we do. Blackpool 0 Burnley 1.

Monday 21 April 2014
Burnley v Wigan

Finally, this could be the day. The big day.

It's Burnley v Wigan, the third-to-last game of the season, and we know now that regardless of what anybody else does, a win for the Clarets will see us promoted.

I sit on my back deck with Radio Five Live on (we're the featured game) and a pint mug of tea (one of the free ones you get from Sports Direct).

We get ahead before half-time through a superb goal from Ashley Barnes, and Kightly seals it with a second later in the game. As the clock runs down I start to feel a rare emotion as a Burnley fan – relaxed. Completely. I'm in no doubt at all that we've won the game and are going up. It's the way it's gone this season – we've been ruthlessly efficient and just aren't going to blow it now. Sure enough the whistle goes, the crowd noise gets louder and the commentators do too to get above them. Something doesn't feel right and I can't put my finger on it.

Am I jealous? I can hear 17,000 people singing and I want to be one of them. Any of them. Anywhere in that ground with a belly full of ale and singing my heart out. I don't want to be here – in my garden in Bangor, with my cup of tea and my cancer.

The last time we were promoted in 2008/09 couldn't have been more different … against the odds we'd finished fifth under Owen Coyle and then beaten Reading 3-0 over two legs to reach the play-off final against Sheffield United. The way we got promoted was different – it was more of a Roy of the Rovers one-off fluke than the fully deserved yet equally unexpected promotion of 2014.

And my involvement in it was also very different. Back then, I didn't have any Northern Irish kids, so was going to a lot of home games regardless. Plus, I didn't have cancer during the run-in. I managed to get to maybe a dozen games that season, including an incredible play-off second leg away at Reading. Due to a narrow selection of flights, I took about two days going to that one – it was well worth it though as two wonder strikes from Martin Paterson and Steve Thompson gave us a 2-0 win.

The final, though, was something else. Me and our Jim (together with my dad and my uncle Tony) made a weekend of it. Our Jim had emigrated to Cayman Islands the previous October, which basically meant he was earning a load of money tax-free (there is no income tax in Cayman) and that he found central London relatively cheap. So he was flashing the cash and I was a welcome beneficiary. The night before the game was a good one – ending up being driven round Soho on one of those bikes ridden by a French student, bellowing out Burnley songs, before being resoundingly ripped off in a strip bar (we'd lost my dad and Tony by this stage) and knocking back a couple of bottles of champagne in the hotel. When I woke the next morning around 7.30am there was a half-full bottle of champagne (now warm and losing its fizz) on the dressing table. Might as well start early – I picked up the Moet by the scruff of its neck and got back on it.

Another bottle was ordered for breakfast and I was pissed before I'd even got to the black pudding. Just after 9ish me and our Jim decided it was time to get to the ground (that being Wembley) and we were in a pub before 10am. It must have just opened as we were the only ones in. Gradually, pockets of Burnley fans arrived and I coined my phrase of the morning, 'hey up, cavalry's arrived' every time a group of Burnley fans walked in, even if it was two old dears in their 60s. After a good four or five hour 'soak' the game was a bit of a blur, although I do remember the winning goal, scored early on in the 12th minute by Wade Elliott.

We carried on after the game, getting back to the hotel around midnight (just me and our Jim by then). He ordered a couple more Moets. I told him I wanted beer still and ordered myself ten bottles of Peroni, which he duly paid for.

The challenge of the next morning and the attempt to get across to Stansted for my flight to Belfast City was not easy. There were tubes and trains involved, timetables, payments, and all sorts of difficulties, mainly derived from the fact that I was nursing a two-day hangover and was in desperate need of a toilet (I normally avoid it but I got good value for that 20p at Liverpool Street).

As I walked off the steps of the plane at Belfast City, still wearing yesterday's clothes – a beer-stained replica shirt, three-quarter-length shorts and white trainers – I felt an immense sense of pride. Like a returning soldier who had just won the war.

It felt amazing.

In comparison, 2014 feels sad and lonely.

I'm delighted like, but I'm … I'm what?

I'm empty. It's over now. It's not even like we can go for the title and catch Leicester. The finish line is behind me and I can't see what's coming next. Five more rounds of RCHOP. Whoopee doo to that. Come on Sean, could you not have strung this out a bit longer? Did you have to be so ruthlessly efficient?

Because I've let this take over me, it occupies my mind all the time; the next game, the team news, the form guide, the odds, everything. It's gone now. Two more exhibition games, which mean nothing. There's the World Cup to look forward to. But the problem with that is that I'm English. And the Premier League – August – it's four months away – four months of being a useless idle bastard with cancer.

Wednesday 23 April 2014

St George's Day. I've stopped being such a dick now. There's always something to play for. We can't let this peter out and not turn up for two games. We need to carry some momentum into the Premier League. Let's finish off without defeat. Two games; home against Ipswich and away against Reading.

It's a funny week. It should have been a chemo one but it's not because of the bank holiday. I'm still fucked off about that. I want that shit in me now so badly. Bring it on, I love that chemo juice.

I decide to do a bit of gardening. The garden is larger than I would like, the grass is longer than I would like and the trees are too big. I can't affect the size. I can cut the grass, so I do. It takes me ages. I've lived here for a year now and have hardly cut it. The trees are a tough one. I convince myself I can do something with tree branches if I have some rope to pull them with. Except that obviously I don't have any rope.

The nice thing about being off work with nothing to do is that being out of something that you don't even really need (i.e. rope, for instance) gives you a task. Something to achieve. To fill the day. Like being retired, I guess. Oh, brilliant, I'll go rope shopping.

There's a DIY store in Bangor that I've walked past a few times but never been in. It's a proper DIY shop like they used to be. Fuck B&Q and Homebase. This shop is for real men. If my dad lived in Bangor he would fucking love it. My problem with it is intimacy. I feel uncomfortable shopping somewhere so personal, where the staff want to help. But to hell with it. I've got cancer, it's now or never, so I take the plunge. I enter and it's clear as day I don't know where the rope is. I'm pointed upstairs. I didn't even know it had an upstairs, this is exciting. The till/desk is near the top of the stairs and the chap there is looking at me as I ascend – the attention – it's just too much.

I make the first move, 'Where's the rope mate?' I ask casually, like I don't even give a fuck if there is no rope.

'There,' he says, pointing to a place a bit too close to where we are standing for me not to look like a bit of a dick.

There is shitloads of rope, on reels. It's charged by the metre, and there are all different thicknesses to choose from. It's the opposite from Homebase where there would be a standard length and standard width, neither of which you wanted, and a premium price to match. It's only 50p per metre. Bloody hell, I could end up buying a load of rope here if I'm not careful.

I notice a presence nearby, what the fuck is that? Oh Jesus, it's an employee. He's on me. He wants to know what I want the rope for. I want him to leave me alone and let me make the wrong choice on my own. We decide on a rope together. It's blue. Not that the colour makes a difference to me. But most of the rope is blue. I didn't expect that. I thought it would be rope-coloured. Like a dirty white. He wants to know how much I want. I've not got a clue. Thing is I can't quite picture how I'm going to use this rope, I just feels like it might be useful in cutting tree branches. I tell him I'll take 20 metres. He pulls it off the reel like a pro and takes it up to the counter.

The chap at the counter grins at me, looks at the rope and says jollily, 'What are you doing? Hanging yourself?' Then he starts chuckling to himself.

A couple of things occur to me.

First, if he makes that joke to everybody buying rope, and he's worked here forever and will continue to work here forever, sooner or later, if he hasn't already, he will say that to somebody who is actually planning to hang themselves.

Second, do people hang themselves with blue rope? I mean, it's blue? It just doesn't feel appropriate. You'd want something a bit more sombre, wouldn't you?

Saturday 26 April 2014
Burnley v Ipswich Town

The game is live on Sky gain. It's one of those that when they did the TV schedule a few weeks back would have looked like an important game but it's not; we're already up and Ipswich can't go anywhere.

It feels like a pre-season friendly. Kightly scores again – his third in as many games – to put us 1-0 up just a few minutes into the second half. And that's how it finishes. Another win. Another clean sheet. Well done Burnley.

The Ipswich manager, Mick McCarthy, in describing Burnley's goal, makes reference to 'Jonny on the spot'. Mick – what are you on about?

I'm delighted we've won this game. It's a strange one, playing a match after you've already been promoted. Our last three promotions have all happened in the last game of the season (two of which were play-off wins). In fact, the last time Burnley were involved in a match like this was Rochdale away in 1991/92.

We'd already won the league and all the other fixtures had been completed; this was one that due to dodgy pitches and postponements hadn't been played, so it was a Tuesday night away game, after the season had ended, with Burnley having nothing to play for.

Despite that, and even though Rochdale could have still made it into the play-offs, we outnumbered the home fans, occupying the full terrace down the side of Spotland as well as behind the goal. As always, it felt like we were occupying the whole world.

The Burnley fans were in great voice and being creative. The repertoire that night included one I'd not heard before, which I assumed had been penned especially for the opponents. It went: 'At least we don't, at least we don't, at least we don't shag our kids. At least, we do-o-n't shag our kids.'

I knew what the words meant but I had no idea why we were singing it at Rochdale. I didn't ask. I just joined in. As you do when you're ten.

Burnley won easily 3-1, with our right-back Ian Measham getting himself a goal for the first time all season.

Monday 28 April 2014
Me v Chemo Two

A week later than I planned, and yes I'm still angry about that, a wee bit anyway, it's back for chemo number two. It's been a full four weeks since I've had a medical appointment of any description. Again, not how I imagined chemo. It's a bit like having a league game and then the international break, and then an FA Cup round but your team's been knocked out so you've no match, and you're chomping at the bit to get back at it.

The sun is shining. It's not that warm but it's blue skies. It looks nice on the eye. What I call good looking weather. Regardless of the weather outside I know for sure that the McDermott Unit will be roasting. I'm prepared this time. I'm going on my own for a start. It's far easier from a life perspective. And I've got the shorts on. It doesn't surprise me that I'm the only punter in the waiting room with their legs out.

Traditionally, I've got hairy legs. It didn't occur to me that the chemo would blast those hairs as well. Come to think of it, when I think of cancer and chemo and hair and all that I picture a woman wearing a bandana. I'm more annoyed about the hairs on my legs than on my head. It's not all my legs – my thighs are intact. As are my arms. But it's my calves. They are unnaturally smooth. It's the only bit people can see as well. I feel like explaining it, I don't know who to, 'Just for the avoidance of doubt, I've not waxed my legs, but I'm actually having chemo, and that's why I've not got hairs on my calves. I usually have a lot of hairs, you should have seen them. They were really good.'

I'm called in quickly enough and brought to the chemo room. I bounce in like a man who's just been promoted. No shorts in here either. Why am I not surprised? I bet this lot have never even heard of Dyche. Lol. I get my chair in the corner. The odd one out, the green one. I can feel myself finding a rhythm that you get with familiarity.

And then they vary it. After they take my bloods they send me back to the waiting room. It seems that this is the norm and last time wasn't. They treated me special on my first visit and let me have the chair for an extra half hour or so. I'm back in the waiting room. *Bargain Hunt* is blaring and the coffee machine being cursed at by geriatrics who couldn't work a bathroom lock. Love it. My only concern is getting my chair back. I hope nobody has swiped it.

I need not worry. I'm called back in and reclaim my throne, which is sat empty.

I fly through the pre-meds and rituximab is given by rapid infusion. The old dear to my right is on the slow treatment. I feel like I'm in the elite club. The fast-track queue at the airport. Stand back ladies and gents for the lad in the shorts who's just been promoted. I'm tearing up the left-hand side of that tube station escalator like a proper London commuter going somewhere fast.

I get a smell of lunch hitting my stomach. But I'm older now, wiser, better at my craft. So when they ask me if I want lunch I know that the correct answer is 'no, I would rather drink a cup of my own semen than that soup you gave me last time'.

I say 'No thanks, I'm okay', which I figure is a milder version of saying the same thing. They'll know what I mean.

No rest for the wicked. The chemo magic juices come down from the pharmacy, and I get on it. The pharmacy chap doesn't appear this time. My take home bag/satchel (it's massive) does though. They tell me if I've concerns or questions to let them know and they'll send him down. I just have the one question. What in God's name is that mouthwash you've given me? That mouthwash. It's like pouring petrol in my mouth. He comes down sharpish with an alternative.

They have given me another supply of laxatives. Why are they doing this? I haven't used any of the first batch. I'm assuming I'm only supposed to be using these if I need to. It's not on my homework timetable anyway. I could sell these. Or stockpile them and have a crazy disco one night.

By 1pm I'm all done. It's all gone like clockwork. Easy! Easy! Easy! Can we play you every week? My father-in-law will pick me up when I call him. But I haven't bothered yet. I've things to do. I head across the road to McDonald's. It's not quite the same as it was before but it definitely beats the soup.

Saturday 3 May 2014
Reading v Burnley

It's Reading away. We've finished second in the league. They are currently sat sixth and in the play-off spots, but if they don't win today there's a chance they'll slip out. It has to mean more to them that it does to us so it's going to be tough, but the last thing we want to do is end on a downer. A draw will do. Let's avoid defeat at least. In a game where we have nothing to play for, many Burnley teams of my childhood/youth would roll over and you'd be expecting an easy home win. Things are different though these days. It's a Sean Dyche Burnley team. It took a while to understand this but we know now what that means is that we're always going to try to win.

We concede early on to a Kieran Trippier own goal, but we're soon level through Scott Arfield. A few minutes later Danny Ings makes it 2-1 to Burnley. It's Ings's first goal since the Bastards away game following his injury and I'm delighted for him. He's bounced back. I love a bouncer backer.

In the second half Reading get it back to 2-2 and that's how it ends. Well done Burnley. It's another good away point, not like we need it. But why not want the points? It looks to be enough for Reading as well. Except it's not. At the City Ground in Nottingham 100 miles away, Brighton grab an injury-time winner against Forest. Brighton finish sixth and Reading seventh.

It's a bit embarrassing for Reading. Their fans are on the pitch celebrating a play-off spot. But they haven't got one. Reading fans run towards the Burnley end feigning a desire to start some trouble. Eh? Reading? Yeah right. They're delighted when a line of stewards block their path.

My only-ever visit to the Madejski came in another promotion-winning season, 2008/09, when we played them in the Championship play-offs. It was only five years ago, but feels like a lifetime. Come to think of it, January this year feels like a lifetime ago. I could get on a plane without having to seek medical advice for a start. Freedom. At the time Reading had Steve Coppell in charge, a man of Premier League pedigree, and they'd been relegated from the Premier League the season before after a two-year stay. They were a top bet for an automatic return and disappointed to only reach the play-offs. Burnley on the other hand were just delighted to be invited to the play-off party.

We'd already scraped a 1-0 victory in the home leg, but our away form had been dodgy. So whilst we were up in the tie, Reading were still favourites to reach the final at Wembley. We'd no expectations, we'd last been relegated from the top flight of English football in 1976, over 30 years ago, and never looked like getting back. Reading felt Premier League, with their new big spaceship of a ground, and had even managed to nick our star player off us a couple of years earlier in Glen Little. But they were entitled to. They'd no history like we did and I can't stand grounds like that (you can't even call it a ground, it's more of an arena), but right then in 2009 they were bigger. So 0-0 at half-time and we were delighted, 45 minutes to hold on and we'd be Wembley bound.

And then from out of nowhere Martin Paterson put us 1-0 up on the night with the best goal of his career and the away end erupted. A few minutes later sub Steven Thompson made it 2-0 with the best goal of his career and we were in dreamland. Reading were done. Even the mighty Glen Little could do nothing about it. And Coppell looked a broken man. Take me back there to that away end. That was some feeling.

What now then? Because now it is well and truly over. If the Wigan game was the last song of the night, well, right now, the DJ has packed up and the bar staff are pushing me out the door.

Saturday 10 May 2014

The most disturbing thing about the hair loss is definitely nothing to do with the hair on my head. For years I have been intrigued as to why the urinals in pubs (or any public place) seem to be such a magnet for pubic hair. And to be fair I find it horrid. In fact, if I see a urinal which is plastered in pubic hair I will move over to the next one. It's even worse than seeing chewing gum amidst those yellow (or sometimes blue, or even green) cleaning tablets. I should add then when I say 'urinal' I am referring to the individual, wall-mounted white ceramic pot (usually

Armitage Shanks branded) as opposed to the communal 'trough' or the communal 'to-the-floor' (sometimes called 'let's get it everywhere, especially on your shoes'). As I say that, I recall the old away end at Luton Town's Kenilworth Road ground. There was basically a room (and I think it was a room in a terraced house which formed the away end) which had a GENTS sign outside; only when you got inside did you realise it was lacking infrastructure. No cubicles. No urinals. No sinks. Just a concrete floor. Basically just a room. I tried to aim upwards to the lights but couldn't reach.

I digress. Back to pubes.

Now, I have never been much of a moulter.

So you can imagine how horrified I was when I realised that I in fact was now a contributor to the pube pile in the pub urinal. I felt awful, and did my best to get the deserters down the drain. As for the ones that couldn't be shifted (the ones falling on the front exterior of the pot rather than in it, 'front fallers') I'm afraid I had to leave them behind. I did think about wiping them off with a tissue but realised (i) that would be rank and (ii) if anybody saw me wiping down a urinal they would think I was a bit of a strange lad.

Tuesday 13 May 2014

I had a thought a while back that I needed a hobby. I haven't been physically active for years. I'm nearly 33. I have it in my head that I haven't been active since I moved to Northern Ireland aged nearly 26. But when I think about it in more detail (i.e. for more than 30 seconds) it's clear that's actually not true. Since I graduated from Nottingham aged 21 I haven't really done anything. Literally, played five-a-side maybe five times, and a few 11-a-side games. Actually, I signed for a Sunday League team at some point between

2002 and 2006, but I stopped playing for reasons I can't remember.

I'm assuming here that I was some sporting type at uni but that's actually bollocks as well. I played 11-a-side hall football in first year a fair bit, and in second and third years I played five-a-side semi-regularly at the JJB soccer dome at Pride Park, but apart from that I just drank cider.

So when I work back from that it's probably the case that I haven't been fit and active since I left sixth form. In fact, I had a minor operation in December of upper sixth, so it's probably more accurate to say I haven't been active since I was 17 and a half.

Actually, I remember that in upper sixth I never actually felt fit at all because I'd been drunk the entire summer before. So let's make it 17.

That's, like, nearly half my life ago. When I was diagnosed one of the first things I did was look into the causes, and, like with a lot of cancers, it's causeless. The only thing you can possibly blame, so to speak, are the general risk factors, and so I'd like to improve my general fitness.

Football has always been my sport, but I think at almost 33 I'm too old to start playing 11-a-side football again, and not sure whether a casual five-a-side is what I'm looking for.

I need something that involves some personal investment/commitment from me (i.e. I need to be locked in to an extent, otherwise, when I go back to work, I'll drop it quickly). For example, golf would work – I'd need to buy equipment and that sort of stuff, even membership, so you'd need to use it. Problem is I'm no golfer. My Uncle Tony and my other grandad were keen golfers. My mum wanted us to be. I started golf lessons when I was seven. I was truly shit at it. I couldn't hit the thing. I didn't like it, and I was crap, and it was expensive. I retired before I turned eight.

I've ruled out the gym. I've had a gym membership before and found it was a complete waste of time. It was a very nice gym, but probably too nice. So when I drove back to Burnley from a day at work in Manchester, it was all too tempting for the workout to consist of jacuzzi, sauna, bar. It was a nice bar with a view overlooking the pool, so often I would take on some Stella Artois at the end of my session. They also did nice cheeseburgers. They sold freshly squeezed orange juice as well. I think they were the first place in Burnley to sell it – I didn't buy any.

So anyway, the missus and I discuss the different types of activities and sports I could get involved in. Mainly the contenders are ones where we already know somebody involved – it's much easier access that way.

When she mentions airsoft though (yes airsoft, you might have to google it – I did), I decide that enough is enough. I'm going to have to be a bit braver.

Define brave. It's hard. I want to be brave. But I don't want to have to speak to anybody. I want to click a faceless button on a screen and hope it happens for me. Except that is bullshit. It never happens that way. I'm going to have to have a conversation. I have to take some action here. I've known that for a long time – if you do something – something else might happen – like a ripple effect. But unless you start by doing something, well then nothing happens.

It was June 1992. The marvellous and memorable 1991/92 season had just come to an end. I was not quite 11. One late midweek afternoon, the 'phone' rang. This was pre-mobile phones. The only phone in the house was the landline. If that sounds daft, the way I answered it was even dafter.

'Hello, Burnley 31326.'

Now what was that all about? I was answering the phone like I was working as an air traffic controller! I have since asked about and am assured that this was a reasonably standard way of answering a landline back then.

It got even stranger though. The much older voice of the male caller told me that he wanted to speak to Michael. I told him that he had the man (boy) and then he said:

'Michael, this is Frank Teasdale, chairman of Burnley Football Club.'

Now, why would the chairman of Burnley FC be phoning the home of a ten-year-old boy? What events had led to this?

Exactly, *The Shrinking of Treehorn*. I have no idea what it was about. It was a book, I remember that much; it had pages and words but that aside I have no memory of it.

The *Burnley Express* is 'the' Burnley newspaper. The people of Burnley loved buying it; to read about Burnley FC, see where else in Burnley they might want to live, and to see who had died that week. Everybody bought the *Burnley Express*, especially the weekend edition on a Friday. At school, we had to read a book each month, and then write a one-page review of it. It was part of a monthly competition run by the newspaper in conjunction with the local primary schools. Completely pointless. Not only do you want me to read a book, you now want me to write about it.

So one afternoon in June 1992, I was playing football out the back with my mate Liam, and the *Burnley Express* just turned up, unannounced, reporter and photographer, a bit like the mafia. I was in the middle of a one-on-one that had been going on for a good two hours, wearing my Burnley shirt with my hair looking like a scarecrow, but they snapped away regardless. And then they interviewed me. I got off on it. I'd never been interviewed before, and, from reasonably irrelevant questions, managed to deliver the most pro-Burnley FC and anti-Bastard Rovers FC interview in the history of the world. The interview, word for word, plus the accompanying photos, appeared in the *Burnley Express* the following Friday, where I was crowned June 1992 winner of the Junior Readers' Club Award for my review of *The Shrinking of Treehorn*.

Everybody in Burnley saw it. Including Burnley FC chairman Frank Teasdale, who seemingly loved it. And that's why he was phoning me.

No grooming intended (although my hair could have done with some). Just a chairman being a proper nice bloke with a young supporter. He even sent me a letter in the post with some player-issue merchandise from the previous year's tour of Russia. Randomly, Burnley had done a pre-season tour in Russia ahead of 1991/92. I later learned the players didn't get much food and lost one stone each.

I saw Frank a few years back in a pub near Clitheroe, around 2000. He was wasted and ended up getting chucked out. I spoke to him as well about the Burnley match earlier that day. I wish I'd thanked him then – that would have been the right thing to do. I regret that. He's dead now. But thanks Frank.

Time to do something. I find a telephone number on the Irish FA website for the local grassroots development officer. I feel proper awkward. How do I even introduce myself? Hello, my name is Michael Heinicke. Hi, it's Michael Heinicke. Or Mr Heinicke? Does he even need to know my name? It's not a work call. Chill out. He answers. I explain my predicament. We come up with a plan. I'm going to be a football coach. Just like Dyche.

Wednesday 14 May 2014

Here we go then. It's all happening fast. But I've nothing to wear. I bought some football shorts and socks and astro trainers recently. Well, in 2007, just seven years ago. Where has the time gone? I find them. They'll do, just. What else though? I'm going to look like one of those older blokes playing five-a-side that never plays normally and has only turned up because they're short of numbers, and looks like he's playing a different sport (shot-putting perhaps) and everyone thinks 'yeah, he was a bit crap', and it might be just based on appearances. But I don't want to be that guy.

Can I just wear a Burnley shirt? Maybe? I don't know. What will other people wear? I take a trip down to JD sports in Bangor. There's a Northern Ireland Adidas hoodie reduced to half price. Can I wear that or will it look like I'm trying too hard? It will do. I get dressed hours before I need to leave. It doesn't look that bad. Black Umbro trainers and white Umbro socks, with white Adidas shorts and a black Adidas hoodie. I don't mind mixing brands; makes me look casual. I look alright actually. I feel quite good. I will blend in, I think.

I leave in ample time to drive to Ballymena. Or Cullybackey as I believe it's called. I've never been there before. That's another crazy-sounding Northern Irish place. It should take me about an hour to get there so I know when I'm nearly there. It starts to get familiar. I pass a bus factory and a country hotel that I know very well. I know exactly where I am. But I don't know where the football pitch is round here.

I've been to a wedding around this way. It was 2006. My wife was a bridesmaid and I didn't know a soul. She was in one of the wedding cars, I was driving on my own in a hire car. It was pre-smartphone, so my plan was to find the hotel (the one I've just passed on the road) by following other cars leaving the church. I backed the wrong horse though. Two wrong horses in fact. I was the third of three cars to pull up outside a tiny B&B. It wasn't right. I wound the window down to speak to one of the chaps getting out of the cars. They were at the same wedding as me, but staying elsewhere. I raced back to the church to find another car to follow. There was nobody there. I asked a passer-by for directions. He was heading in the same direction. Get in then lad. He was carrying a holdall. At that point I didn't live in Northern Ireland – the sight of a man from NI with a closed holdall scared me. He might be trying to blow me up. Just like they did with that royal fella Mountbatten.

Anyway, it's the same hotel.

Up a dirt track on the other side of a road is a big barn. It looks like a farm building.

I pull up outside and know I'm in the right place when the Irish FA guy Wes gets out of the car next to me and starts unloading his gear. Football gear. Those balls look delicious.

I'm the first person there, apart from Wes. We'd spoken on the phone yesterday and he remembers the English bloke with the last-minute booking. He shows me inside and up the stairs into a small function room. One of the walls is largely glazed and looks on to the five-a-side 3G pitch below. Wow. It's beautiful. I had no idea what to expect from Cullybackey Sports Hut but I love this. In fact I want one. Wes explains that it was a farm building that was surplus to requirements, so they did this to it.

Amazing. Took something crap and made it great. I love that. It's romantic. Victory from the jaws of defeat. The negative into the positive. It's where I'm at now. I don't tell Wes my predicament. He can just think I have a shiny head and bald calves.

The first half of the three-hour grassroots intro course is classroom-based. There's a good 30 or so people who have turned up, around a third of which are female primary school teachers. A lot of the males are in packs of two and three, wearing matching club gear. It looks like I'm the only singleton there. It doesn't take very long for Wes to persuade me that kids' football is not like it was when I was a lad. I'd expected to be shy and sit quietly in the corner, but I can't help myself. I'm reminiscing at a hundred miles an hour. I start contributing to the discussion, and I get into storytelling mode.

My football career was only a junior one, I'm not mixing it up with anything I experienced as an adult. I remember it vividly. I compare and contrast. The ball. One ball between 20 kids or 20 balls between 20 kids? He's right, there were never enough balls. Ah, but at Blackburn Rovers there was. Have I really only just noticed that?

Child protection didn't exist when I was younger. Wes tells us that we shouldn't join in playing with kids. I think about one of my former coaches. He didn't join in exactly. He'd play his own games. For instance, lining up a wall of 12-year-olds for a free kick and belting the ball at them from ten yards. As in, intentionally hitting the wall. I don't think he had sadistic tendencies. I genuinely think he was trying to help us, make us tougher or something. Maybe it worked. Who knows? He got me enough times. We trained on one of those old-style astroturf pitches, the hard bouncy ones where you might be able to play hockey (don't know, never played it) but you've never been able to play football. He once knocked me clean off my feet and I was still moving as I hit the deck, and ended up with those horrible friction burns on my knees. It would be laughable these days.

Wes talks about parents being ultra-competitive and putting too much pressure on their kids. I think that's always been a problem. Not my own dad. If anything I wouldn't have minded him putting a bit more pressure on me.

Other parents were mental. There was a team we used to play against in the Hyndburn League, and the right-winger's dad would literally run down the wing with him. Not on the pitch, on the other side of the touchline. Sheer lunacy.

The difference I think is that there is more of it now. More teams, more leagues, and much, much younger kids. So whatever problems we had in the 1990s, it's kind of multiplied.

Being on the pitch feels fantastic. He takes us through a few drills. He doesn't need 30 participants, somewhere between 8 and 12 depending on the drill; the rest watch and take notes. I don't take any as I make sure I'm always playing. I give it everything I have. My touch feels good and my passing is sharp. We do some one-on-ones, some shooting drills, and I'm treating it like a World Cup Final. It might only be a grassroots course in a converted barn somewhere outside of Ballymena, and there might only be ten primary school teachers watching, but I still get a buzz when that ball hits the back of the net. They all count. I never scored enough goals. I've goals in me yet.

It flies by. I don't want it to end. Relentless. Just like Burnley. Wes must think I'm on drugs. I am as it happens, but not the ones he's thinking of. This is therapy. I feel 100 per cent alive.

I pay my £30 as I'm leaving at the end of the session. £30. £30. The best money I've ever spent.

I get home and get on the internet, and look up the next Level One course. It's six weeks away.

Monday 19 May 2014
Me v Chemo Three

This is the mid-season slog that I was worried about. Chemo number three.

For whatever reason it's slow going today and I'm waiting around longer than usual. 'Usual', what am I, a chemo veteran now?

Luckily, though, the waiting room at the McDermott Unit really does craic me up and has a hidden entertainment value. I've been in here a few times now. It's full of old folk.

There's a couple of great features. The coffee machine for a start. It's not funny. It's just a coffee machine. But put it in with this clientele and all of a sudden you've got live comedy happening all over the shop. They look at it as though it's landed from outer space. Some do a sideways head turn in 45-degree segments and move their eyes to lock on a like-minded old timer who they can share their bemusement with. Others shrug their shoulders and simultaneously turn their hands to reveal their palms, but the answers aren't there.

It starts with selecting the pod from the drawer. There's a choice and that can be difficult when you just want 'coffee'. Before that, though, it's realising you need to select a pod. And that they're in wee drawers. So I normally go for a Colombian, which the bloke I'm training on the machine is staggered by. I can't tell if he's being racist or thinks I'm being a fancy pants. The thing is though mate, this coffee stuff (yes, even the coffee you used to be able to get in the 1970s and probably still can) does tend to come from South America and Africa, and not the Glens of Antrim.

There are often milk issues too. The milk cartons are kept in a drawer but can they find them? Can they bollocks.

The best bit, though, is once they've cracked it or been shown how to use it (guarantee they'll forget next time) the plastic cup can be a bit too hot to handle. Yes that's right, always whinging it's too cold and then give them some heat and they're too hot. They have those plastic cup holders to pop the cup in. Brown coloured, with a handle. It is blatantly obvious these are for re-using. But no, the bin is overflowing with the cup holders despite signs (yes, signs on the walls amidst the medical advice posters) asking please don't put the cup holders in the bin.

The pile of magazines is like a prop from a TV set. It looks like a nice choice of magazines. Glossy and thick. Get a bit closer though and you realise it's a deception. There are a few of the junk *Woman's Own* type rag full of real life stories where you get £200 for embarrassing yourself with headlines like 'My husband had sex with our hamster but I still forgave him'. But the bulk of the magazine collection is a monthly publication with copies going back for the last two or three years. *Camping and Caravanning Monthly.* I've nothing against somebody buying that magazine. If you own a caravan it makes sense.

The decision, though, that this is the sort of mainstream publication that would work well in a waiting room is optimistic at best.

The TV is better described as a monitor. About 24 inch, mounted high on a wall. I'd say it's only viewable from around 40 per cent of the seats in the waiting room, and even then it requires significant neck craning to see the screen. But you probably wouldn't want to. Because all it shows, all day long, I don't know how, is *Bargain Hunt*.

Finally I get settled in the chemo room in my 'usual' chair in the corner, but I'm already an hour behind last time. Hopefully we can make up some time. Yes, that plane thing again. Let's get ourselves a tailwind.

But it's not happening for me today. It's slow. Once the R is in, the chemo normally is quick. Like an idiot I fall asleep in the chair. They don't attempt to wake me. I'm raging with myself when I wake up.

Now where is my chemo? It's not even arrived. I want my chemo in me. Get it in me now. Plus it's absolutely boiling hot.

I try to get the attention of a nurse, like trying to catch the eye of an air stewardess and asking for a glass of water.

Delays in the pharmacy.

Eventually, the pharmacist arrives with my chemo and take-home goody bag. He asks me whether I've been drinking plenty of water. He'd mentioned this to me before, it's important to drink lots of water when having chemotherapy. I haven't questioned why this is the case but I'm finding that because I have cut down on alcohol I am drinking lots of water anyway without consciously trying. So I tell him that I am and he asks me how much.

'Err, probably about 10 pints', I tell him.

'What? Per day?' he asks.

I nod to indicate that's correct. He raises his eyebrows and opens his mouth and it takes a few seconds for any words to come out.

'Well, you definitely don't need to be drinking any more than that, that's more than enough, and in fact you should probably try to drink a bit less.'

Wow. First they tell me to cut down alcohol and now they're telling me to cut down on the water. I wonder what's next? Finally, I'm done. I get out around 4pm. Three hours later than last time. But I've won. Might only be 1-0 compared to last time's 5-0, but it's done, and in the bag. A win is a win. I've three of these in me, halfway there.

Tuesday 20 May 2014

I wake up feeling much the same as the first two. I head to the en-suite for a good morning slash and as I do so I feel liquid running down my leg. I'm obviously half asleep and pissing all over myself. Except I'm not. I check my aim and flow and look at my leg. The liquid is brown. Nice one, I've just shit myself.

I wipe the liquid up, keep on my soiled (yes, soiled) boxer shorts, and casually walk downstairs. I rinse them in the sink in the utility room and think of somewhere to hide them. I hang them to dry in the garage next to a couple of woodsaws.

I've come close to shitting myself at a football match.

In the late 1980s there was still violence in football. It was probably on the decline but still there, and Burnley had their share of it. By the time I got my first season ticket at the start of the 1988/89 season, we were the biggest club in the Fourth Division in terms of traditions and history, had the biggest ground, the biggest home attendances and the biggest away followings.

We were a big draw for some of the village teams in the division, and the villagers would come out in force to pit their wits against the big boys. One such team was Lincoln City. It was on an away trip to Lincoln in 1989/90 that I learnt a lesson about the word 'city'. Even a village can be called a 'city' if there is a cathedral in it. It's one of those great English traditions that makes no sense anymore, even if it once did. Should every town with a Premier League team be a city, or every town with a stadium holding more than 20,000 seated?

My dad always took us to seated away sections, primarily because it would give small people a better view, but also because he saw it as safer from any 1980s football violence that might arise. The set-up at Lincoln gave away fans a section of terracing down the side and half of the seats behind one goal, so that the allocation was given as an L shape in the corner. The seated area had some shallow trench-type terracing beneath it which was no longer in use. We took our seats on the front row, to the left-hand side of the goal. In front of us was the gangway and then the front wall, beneath which was a 10ft drop to the trench below.

Segregation in seated stands was a bit different to the large fences on the terraces. It was normally a line of stewards, but on this occasion it was more like a dotted line with very few dots. Before the game had kicked off I had noticed a lot of walking up and down the aisles on the Lincoln side of the divide, and looking over at the Burnley fans. One lad in particular stood out – he was wearing a scarf covering his face and a red-and-black checked lumberjack jacket. He looked like a right nobhead.

Even though I knew something was odd, I wasn't prepared for what happened a few minutes into the game. I first noticed the movement on the right-hand side from the Lincoln fans, as lumberjack and his friends charged down the steps to the front and ran down the gangway towards the Burnley fans. From out of my left eye I saw a larger group of Burnley fans charging in the opposite direction towards the Lincoln fans. They met in the middle and boots and fists went flying. There was maybe only 15 or so in total at it, but the width of the gangway was only about two metres, bordered on one side by the front wall and on the other side by a seven-year-old me. I shit myself (but not literally that time). They say these moments are fight or flight. I did neither. I just sat still crying. To say that this was happening near me is an understatement. They were touching me. Not touching distance, they were actually touching me. Lumberjack boy was being grappled by a Burnley supporter who was much bigger than him, wearing all denim, a thick black belt with a golden buckle and long curly hair – he looked a bit like one of our players at the time, Tony Hancock, but it couldn't have been him because he was on the pitch, albeit probably doing far less damage to the opposition. Denim man's leg was literally on mine as he crunched lumberjack boy into a headlock.

A couple sat behind asked, 'Is that lass okay?' as I was lifted to the safety of the next row. I was distraught. I had short hair and looked nothing like a girl, but my wimpy reaction to this violence had made some fellow Burnley fans think I was a girl. I cried even more.

The stewards were soon joined by police, who restored calm. We got beat 1-0 but I remember nothing of the game. But at least I didn't actually shit myself.

Friday 23 May 2014

It's Catherine's work summer ball at the Titanic building. I only had my chemo on Monday and even though a couple of months back I'd have thought there is no way I could attend something like this, I feel okay still so have decided to go.

For clarity, I really don't want to. These things are bad enough when you hardly know anybody, and if you're not drinking much then it's even worse. But I don't want to not go either. I don't want to be the husband who can't make it because he's sick with cancer.

I decide beforehand that to limit my drinks I will make a note on my phone of everything I have. I am working on the basis that this will, in some way, regulate or normalise me.

It starts at 7.30pm and is finished by 1am. I can still operate my phone, which I suppose is a good sign. Scores on the doors as follows:

2 glasses champagne
3 glasses red wine
1 glass white wine
4 pints Guinness

1 Bushmills
1 Brandy
1 Baileys

I'm not sure what Dr Ong would make of that but I'm probably over my 14 units per week. I feel sober. My wife is delighted with my behaviour. Last year at the same event I was a complete mess. Christ knows how much I drank last year.

Monday 26 May 2014

I've had so many medical appointments, some private, some NHS, I'm losing track. I phone my health insurance company to check that they've received and approved all the private ones. The chap on the phone asks me about my ongoing treatment, so I explain to him that I'm having that done on the NHS so there won't be any more private bills.

He asks me if I'm claiming the 'cash payments'. I have no clue what this lad is going on about. It turns out that every time I have an NHS appointment instead of a private one, the insurance company is going to give me £50 – per appointment. Not the NHS, they're going to give the cash to me. So not only am I getting the best treatment in the world for free (which, based on form, I think it is), I'm getting paid to do it.

I'm financially unscathed by cancer. I'm still getting paid in full from work. At the moment I'm probably better off as I'm spending less on fuel and overpriced coffee. To be 'up' feels wrong, but I'll take it. I'm a lucky boy.

The accountant in me starts thinking back to three versus six. The three would have come with radiotherapy, which is a much larger number of shorter appointments. So even if I was only there an hour, bang, £50. I could have cleaned up.

I think about donating the £50s to a charity. I don't need the money. But I don't do that. I book myself on the Level One course.

Wednesday 28 May 2014

I'm eating a lot. I'm so hungry. And I'm in the house on my own all day. What else am I to do?

Inspired by my drinking list from the other night, I decide to write down my food and beverage intake for the day.

Today's takings are:
Shreddies with half pint milk
2 Scotch eggs
2 Cornish pasties
700g chicken wings
200g beans
Chicken pie
Chips
1 blueberry muffin
1 ring donut
1 cup of coffee
2 cups of tea
1 diet coke
4 pints of water

Well I'm doing well cutting down on the water anyway. Let's take the positives.

Thursday 29 May 2014

29 May rings a bell with me. Was this the day in 2009 when we won the Championship play-off? Or was it the 1994 play-off? Or was it the Sherpa Van in 1988 (we didn't win that)? Can't remember, I'll have to google it later.

Another scan. CT variety. They're checking the progress. Half-term report. From the outside it looks like there is nothing to scan. Surely the answer is that this is great. I'm top of the class, am I not?

They've told me to fast for four hours beforehand. The appointment is at 1pm so I'll have to get up early to get some eating done. I don't remember fasting for the CT scan back in February, although that was an unplanned one. Hey, though, maybe I'll get a scone afterwards. Maybe that's why they brought me the scone. I thought it was a 'sorry you've got cancer' scone – a sympathy scone – it could have been standard issue for a CT scan on the presumption you've been fasting.

I doubt I'll be getting a scone though – the NHS isn't great on food. The soup is a slimming technique if ever there was one.

I have a bowl of Shreddies at 8.30am with a coffee. Then I panic because come 9am I can't have any more food until much later this afternoon. So I bring a donut and a blueberry muffin back to bed with me. Classy.

I drive up to the hospital in plenty of time. The car park is rammed as ever, but the queue to get in only takes a few minutes and I get a nice space; one of those where there is a flower bed on the driver side rather than another car.

I say nice but as I open the door I'm greeted by a three-piece dog shit nestled in said flower bed. Bizarre. Who lets their dog have a shit in a flower bed without picking it up? More to the point, who takes their dog for a walk in a hospital car park? There are some strange folk about.

Strange folk in the waiting room as well.

It's a CT scan so there is liquid to be drunk. It's different to the other stuff I've had. It's clear and tastes pretty much like water, much better than that rank milk stuff. Only problem is I need to drink more of it – two litres. But there's an hour to do it and these things are important, so get on with it. Plus, I know I have it in the locker to do a pint every 15 minutes over several hours, so I can handle this.

Not if you're over 70 though. The old lady across from me has been drinking hers for over an hour and still isn't halfway through. She's going to hold up the queue. She starts telling me and another older chap that she's not having any more, then she tells the nurse the same. She can't manage any more and she doesn't like the taste. I think she ought to try the milk; relatively, this stuff is delicious. The nurse tells her to drink two more glasses and that will suffice. The old lady offers her one glass. The nurse tells her 'this isn't a game'.

I think it is a game. That's how I'm treating it anyway. I want to win the game. Relentless. I want to be the Ballon d'Or winner of cancer patients.

Last time I had a CT scan it was on the private medical. They gave me the results whilst I was still strapped to the device. This is the NHS, it's a bit different. Less friendly, is it? No it's not that, it's more risk averse. There is not a chance the lad doing this is going to give me an off-the-cuff reaction to what he sees.

Do I need him to? I don't think I do.

I'm convinced it's fine.

Wednesday 4 June 2014

I've decided that I'm not going to bother phoning Dr Ong to ask for the results of the CT scan. I think it will be grand. And they are what they are, I can't change them. And regardless of what they are, it's not going to change my treatment. So, what if the cancer is still there, what is going to happen? Sure they'll just treat me for cancer which is what they are doing anyway?

I call into the office for the first time in a few weeks. I chat to the lad who had told me about his mum's treatment being a success.

He asks me whether I'm having any side effects and I tell him no. He pushes me on this:

'What? None? No sickness or anything? Really?'

I tell him I feel 100 per cent fine. Nothing at all.

'Oh well,' he continues, 'the drugs have probably moved on since my mum was having chemotherapy.'

I gather from this that his mum did have some adverse side effects. I think he did mention that before.

'How long ago was that?' I ask him.

I don't expect the answer that I get.

'Well, my mum's been dead for ten years so yes, it was just over ten years ago.'

Dead, she's dead? I thought he told me how well it went?

I'm completely confused by what this lad has just told me.

'Sorry mate, I didn't realise your mum was dead. But, I thought you told me her treatment was successful?'

'Well,' he says, 'yes it sort of was, the chemotherapy got rid of the cancer for sure, there's no doubt about that.'

'So what did she die of then?'

'Well, yes, the chemotherapy sort of caused all her organs to shut down completely, she stopped eating, and eventually died.'

A few months ago when I was diagnosed every man and his dog was wanting to tell me their cancer stories. Someone they knew had a different type of cancer, completely bearing no resemblance to mine. For example '...and they died and now live in hell'. Or 'and they lived happily ever after and now own a surf shop in Devon'. This was one of the good ones, a success story. Apparently it wasn't wholly successful.

Not a bit in fact. Had he been selective in what he told me? Or had I been hearing selectively?

Think positive. I'm running my own race. Nobody else's. Kick on.

Friday 6 June 2014

How am I going to get a club now? I don't know where to start. I've lived here seven years and I don't even know any teams, apart from Irish League ones. Disgraceful behaviour from myself.

So that's where I start. I don't do Facebook so I look at the websites of the three Irish League teams nearest to me: Bangor, Ards and Glentoran.

Ards are looking for a manager for their under-19s squad. I can't see any other advertised vacancies. Sod it. I craft an email to the Ards FC chairman expressing my interest in the job. I say job – there actually is some form of payment attached to it. I open it up by acknowledging my lack of experience and saying that I'd be interested in any other coaching roles in the academy. I'm pleased with my email. If I've achieved nothing else, I've made a connection with someone in the position of recruiting coaches into football.

I'm expecting a reply saying no thanks and then either (i) yes we have other positions in the academy or (ii) no we don't.

The response arrives quickly. They want to interview me for the under-19s job next Tuesday night. I wonder has he not read the email right. Did he miss the bit where I talked about having no experience? Or was my footballing CV impressive enough even though it ended 15 years ago when I was still a child? This is funny. It's different. I'm nervous and looking forward to it all at the same time. I'm excited.

Monday 9 June 2014
Me v Chemo Four

I'm busy thinking about the big job interview tomorrow night so I'm not even thinking of the CT scan results.

Because of that, when they call me in from the waiting room, usually just for blood tests, I'm surprised when it's the cancer doctor rather than a nurse that takes me into a private room. My cancer is a blood cancer so I'm looked after by Dr Ong in Haematology, and not a cancer doctor which they called an oncologist. I never knew this a few months ago. It means that Dr Ong is never anywhere near the McDermott Unit. But I see quite a lot of the other doctor, Barbara. There are a number of instances in life where you're only half conscious of somebody and only over time do you realise what they are about, and then you do without anybody telling you. Barbara is a general cancer doctor. She's more user friendly than Dr Ong. As in, I'm not scared of her.

Before I even realise what the subject matter is, she tells me the CT scan was clear. No indication of cancer. Slight markers coming up on my neck which she thinks is scar tissue from the biopsy.

This results thing hasn't happened for me. The build-up, fear, panic, and then boom, you get the result. And its trauma or jubilation. Like on TV. My diagnosis was a bolt from the blue, I had no clue it was going to happen, I wasn't even worried. This result, I wasn't even thinking about it to be worried either way because I knew it was all fine. It's been a bit like Burnley this season. Just like I gradually came to realise that we are in fact getting promoted, this has been the same. I got this in an instant, but this recovery has been a slow realisation that it's happening and, factually, I'm getting over this hurdle. And it's the same approach. I think I'm working hard at cancer. As hard as anybody could do. It's just like Dyche. I'm reaping the rewards, relatively anyway.

Still, I can't resist asking her the question. Are you sure I need to do all six?

I get my usual chair. The day flies in. I fill the hours preparing for my interview tomorrow. This mainly involves me reading through material I've downloaded from the internet. There is tons of material. I'd realised this at the grassroots course with Wes but football has moved on massively since I played it. It definitely looks that way. Either that or all the material is a load of rubbish. I think again about this. I can't help but wonder if I'm overthinking it. But there is loads of focus around technique. It keeps coming back to that, and the British don't have it in the same way other countries do. Ironically, my technique is my best asset, and I've got Rovers to thank for that. Yuck, I can't say thank you to those Bastards. But it's true, I can feel it now nearly 20 years after they kicked me out. 'Practice makes permanent' was what they used to tell us. My brief time there benefitted me. But what did I do with that? Not enough. I'm ready for this interview, anything they ask me on coaching methods or, dare I say it, 'philosophy' I will have an answer for (of sorts). Philosophy – that new Man United manager Louis Van Gaal keeps banging on about it – what is that bloke going on about?

Tuesday 10 June 2014

Ards FC don't have their own ground (they rent from Bangor FC) so the interview takes place in the Ards FC social club in the centre of Newtownards. Even though I only live five miles away, it's not on my way into Belfast; so I'd guess that I've been to Newtownards less than a dozen times in my life. I decide to wear a suit on the basis that you can't be overdressed for an interview and also because it's what Sean would do. I allow plenty of time to get there so that I can find the place. The entrance is squeezed in between two shops at street level and it's just a staircase up to the first-floor club. When I get there the bar is clearly closed – it's empty – there are chairs stacked on tables, and there is a bloke in an Ards FC polo shirt hoovering what looks like a newly installed carpet.

'Brian won't be a minute,' polo shirt man tells me. He wanders off with hoover in tow.

I take a look around the social club, there's some interesting stuff on the walls. A pennant from their 1958 European Cup game against Reims. Burnley also played Reims in the European Cup in the 1960s, 1960/61 in fact, the season after we won the league – I have the programme somewhere. There's a noise on the stairs and a few seconds later a strange-looking chap walks in. He looks at the bar, looks at me. 'Is there no-one serving, mate?' he asks. I can't tell whether he's attempting a joke, drunk or slow. You've never seen a bar look more closed than this, short of having metal shutters in front of the pumps. I tell him they're shut. He says he'll pop back in ten minutes.

A few minutes later polo shirt man reappears, now hooverless. 'Brian's ready for you now,' and he leads me into the chairman's office. Polo shirt man, just as I think he's about to go and put the kettle on, takes a seat at the table. The chairman, wearing a suit, albeit a very light-coloured one, introduces himself and his two fellow directors, one being polo shirt man himself, and the second is a chap already seated who seems to be wearing a Liverpool FC rain jacket.

The chairman delivers the first question: 'So then Michael, do you want to talk us through your experience to date?'

Hmm. Nice question. How do I stretch out the word 'none'? And have they not read the bloody email?

I play it with a straight bat. I run through my footballing CV, which stops in its tracks at age 17. I tell them about the cancer. They are a bit stuck for words. I do my best to try to make it sound historical. As though this was something that's happened to me, but now I'm over it and it's in the past. I tell them that I've had a scan which was clear. I don't use the phrase 'all clear' intentionally, I just let them infer it. And I don't tell them I'm talking about an interim scan, the results of which I only got yesterday.

I tell them, as per my email, on the assumption I don't get the under-19s job, I'd be interested to hear of any coaching opportunities at any level. They agree this is a good idea, and keep coming back to it.

Wednesday 11 June 2014

The email arrives at 9.00 the next morning. As expected I didn't get the job. But they were impressed with my attitude and want to offer me a different role within the club. I take this as a massive victory. I've made a cold contact and it's worked. I read the words 'impressed with your attitude' – I'm glad. It's a compliment. I'll take what I can when I can.

Friday 13 June 2014

I can't wait for England to get their World Cup campaign underway tomorrow. Can we do it? Well we should be good to get to at least the quarters. We haven't managed that since 2006.

The World Cup of 2006 and the Euros two years before blur into one. Probably because Portugal knocked us out on penalties in the quarter-finals of both tournaments.

I watched the 2006 World Cup quarter-final in the Burnley League club (perhaps it was still called the Irish League then). I distinctly remember that because I bumped into my old mate Pete Wood (aka Woody). The place was packed and we watched the game stood up on seats at the back.

We went back to our Jim's house after the game and he took his frustrations out on a tree. One of those short conifers. The tackle was bad, leaving the tree snapped in two. The tree never recovered. It died from its injuries. Cristiano Ronaldo has a lot to answer for.

Saturday 14 June 2014
England v Italy

When I spoke to the chairman during the week he suggested that I call in to the academy's open trials. They are being held at Diary Hall in Newtownards. I nod along my agreement but I've no idea where it is. But I can easy work that out.

My real issue is what to wear. I really don't have the wardrobe for this. I don't have sports clothes. I can't show up in casual shorts and a t-shirt. I need to look a bit more sporty, but without trying too hard. I call into Sports Direct to panic buy some Adidas shorts (with pockets though, that's important) and a Puma polo shirt. That should do it.

I feel like a bit of an idiot just rocking up to this. Luckily the chairman spots me and beckons me over. He introduces me to a couple of lads.

'This is Chris,' he says to me, gesturing to the lad to his left. 'He, err, err, he got the job that you applied for.'

All three of us laugh. It's a good thing it's not a proper job we're talking about.

I'm wondering what this other role they have in mind is. It soon dawns on me that there isn't one specifically. He encourages me to have a look around. I talk to a couple of the committee members. I tell them I'm from Burnley. I'm not sure whether they think I'm from Burnley, as in FC, because they hastily suggest I might want to take on the academy director role. I persuade them I'm not qualified.

There's a couple of pitches where the kids are all young. Different age groups but all under the age of ten. All primary school kids anyway. I dismiss them. I don't want to work with those ones. Why? I think they're probably a bit too close in age to George. I've some sort of issue there which I've not fully put my finger on yet.

There might be a vacancy with the under-15 team. I watch them training. The guy taking the session apparently has had enough and might not be continuing into next season. I like this age group because this is where it went wrong for me. There is where I gave up on the dream. Not that the dream would have necessarily come to anything. But this is when I stopped believing so that I would never know.

I'm looking at the pitch and chatting to one of the parents and I can see several versions of a 14-year-old me. The dad is telling me how they've struggled. They're not big enough and they are getting bulldozed. His lad looks decent. Good feet. But he's small, he can't kick the ball far enough and gets pushed off it.

I was the same. I was young for my school year, so always didn't mind being behind size wise. I had an excuse for that, I was generally younger than the rest of the lads in my year and it makes a difference when you're young. In my last year of primary school I was probably a bit below average, and that was fine. I just barely grew at all for the next four years and fell further and further behind. I ended up as a relative midget. I was 4ft 11in in the first year and still only 5ft 2in at the end of the fourth year. And I wondered why my football was going downhill? Granted, height is only one aspect. I was still a boy though. I was playing against six-foot cavemen with beards (well actually sideburns as it would have been at the time, the beards are a new thing).

It's so easy to get disillusioned. But I can work with lads this age. I can tell them not to worry. Don't worry about getting beat. They'll grow one day, if not upwards, then you'll at least get that bit of testosterone that you need. Then they can measure you.

I make it clear that I'd like to take this group. I like the age, and I like the fact that they're struggling. I love a David against Goliath. One of the committee members interrupts the session to ask the coach whether he's jacking it in. I can't believe that just happened. Perhaps it could have waited until later. He's undecided.

I spend an hour or so and then head on. They need to talk to the academy chairman but they'll be in touch.

The clothing situation is a problem. I phone my mate Carl and ask him to lift me some stuff from work.

England lose 2-1 against Italy. It's a disappointing start to the World Cup. We do well to equalise so soon after going a goal behind but Balotelli gets the winner for Italy early in the second half. Never mind. That was the hardest game, we should still get out of the group.

We need to. I don't really enjoy it unless we get to the quarters, although 1998 was a good World Cup even though England got knocked out in the second round. By that time, I was almost 17, which, in Burnley terms, means you're a veteran of the pubs even though you're still underage.

A group of us walked out of sixth form to watch the first England game in the Woodman pub on Tod Road. Scholes and Shearer scored to give England a 2-0 win against Tunisia and a good start to the campaign. There were recriminations though the next day. The punishments were wide ranging. At one extreme, a lad got expelled. His mistake being leaving empty beer cans in the common room. He was just excited and having a couple of cold ones (well, probably warm) before the game. At the other end, three of us got away scot-free. I can't remember the reason, I think somebody managed to get our teacher that afternoon to give us permission to miss his lesson, after the event. And I just hung on to the coat-tails of whoever had negotiated that deal. I always seemed to get away with it. It's a bit like that song 'I've been getting away with it, all my life'. It's what's happening now I think.

Wednesday 18 June 2014

There's a note through the door telling me I have a parcel to collect from the post office. Good man Carl, he's delivered already.

I hand over the card and the young girl of around 20 goes to locate the package. She returns with a grin on her face. It really is a package. The way he has put the merchandise together looks like a big black cock, all wrapped in layers of black bin liners. Very creative. Had I been home when Royal Mail knocked on the door it wouldn't have been as bad. Our post (woman) would have had to hand it to me but I wouldn't have to walk back to the car with it and strap it in the seat next to me.

I can't resist opening it though. The bollocks are Wolverhampton Wanderers training kit which he has craftily rolled up into two equal-sized balls. He's the first-team physio at

Wolves, it isn't just random. Wolves have their kit produced by Puma and I already know that their standard boot supply (he gets a good few pairs himself) is Puma King. I'm looking forward to having some of these. They're a classic black design with white trim and a lovely fold-over tongue. I've never had any. Our Jim did.

To my horror, the shaft of the package contains a pair of Adidas Predators. Now, I had two pairs of Predators. The first one I preferred; black with the three traditional Adidas stripes down the side in white. Screw-in studded sole. Red fold-over tongue. I loved them. I think I played my best football in them. My second pair were also black with white and red trim, but were a bit more modern-looking and less classic. They were blades rather than screw-in round studs. And the Predator fins weren't as pronounced. That was disappointing because I, unlike many, was of the firm opinion that those things worked. But still, they were black.

What he has sent me here is a monstrosity. It is so far from my vision of a football boot you cannot describe it. Blue. Illuminous electric blue, and orange. The predator fins are virtually non-existent, you need to touch them to even know they're there. The scar on my neck is more of a ridge than those. And for some reason the text 'Lethal Zones' is written on the boot. It's embarrassing. Oh well, they will have to do. And on the plus side I'm getting them for free when they probably cost over £100 to buy. I shouldn't grumble.

My last Burnley away game was Wolves at the end of last season 2012/13. It was a bit of a weird one; we won for a start, but the atmosphere was just horrible, as we effectively relegated Wolves to League One. The weirdest bit though was watching Burnley from the other end. I sat under cover with the Wolves fans.

I had a very good reason for that. I was staying with Carl for the weekend, so I had a free ticket in the main stand, near to, but not in, the directors' box.

Wolves really needed to win. We were looking over our shoulder ourselves and whilst a defeat wouldn't have been the end of the world, a draw would have been a great result.

The atmosphere in the stadium was a tense one, at least it was in the Wolves sections. I looked over to my left at the Burnley fans behind the goal. It was so surreal seeing Burley fans in the minority section, but not being in it.

Crowds influence footballers, just as footballers influence crowds. It can be good or bad. But if you're at home with a big crowd in a vital game, you need the crowd with you.

It was a defining moment for me with Dyche that day. Burnley players looked sure of themselves, calm even. The Wolves lads were clearly nervous. We scored early in both halves, and both times I had an out-of-body-type experience watching the away end rocking up and down – a Burnley away end in full swing. It looked beautiful. Wolves were finished. Even after Burnley had a man sent off and Wolves got a goal back it was done. The crowd got temporarily excited urging Wolves forward but it was too late; it was all too tense and panic stations for Wolves; they lumped a few balls into the box, Burnley batted them back.

The final whistle went and we'd won. I don't know how Dyche did, but he took the emotion out of it, and 90 minutes later, we're safe, and they're doomed. I feared I might be as well. My cover being blown wasn't the problem, the angry mob of Wolves fans who'd invaded the pitch and were heading towards the directors' box were. Not that they got anywhere near them as the directors retreated inside for wine and prawn sandwiches.

A few Wolves fans thought that instead it might be an idea to smash up the dugouts (it's an idea, not a very well thought through one, but an idea nonetheless).

There's a number of clubs like this, where there are massive rifts between owners and fans. We're lucky, we're not at that extreme where the fans are the owners, but at least all our owners are fans.

Thursday 19 June 2014
Uruguay v England

England lose 2-1 to Uruguay, with Suarez scoring a late winner with his second of the game to cancel out Rooney's equaliser.

England are so frustrating. They always leave me feeling completely underwhelmed. It's the opposite to Burnley. The Clarets are punching above our weight, we're overachieving. England … it just ends in disappointment every time.

1990 wasn't like that. I loved that World Cup. We probably did overachieve as well in reaching the semi-finals. We were all proper into England at school. That game against Belgium was especially brilliant, with David Platt scoring a wonder goal in the last minute of extra time to win the game.

I celebrated that goal by taking all my clothes off and dancing around the room. Yes, naked. I wasn't even drinking. I was only eight. I've been waiting 24 years to celebrate another England goal like that. Well the wait goes on. It looks like we're out.

Friday 20 June 2014

I speak to Carl about the boots. It turns out I made my request at the wrong time of year. The season finished a month ago and pre-season hasn't yet started. He couldn't find anything, apart from a pair left behind by a young player who has just left the club to join Tranmere.

Now there's a club having it tough, just having been relegated to League Two (fourth tier). For the first 13 years watching Burnley, they were either at our level or at a level above, normally above us.

The away game at Prenton Park in our single season in Division One (second tier) in 1994/95 was memorable. I'd been there a couple of times before in our Division Four days, but by 1995 they'd redeveloped three sides of it, including the large stand behind the goal, which was split between home and away fans. They were on a different level to us back then, with players like Pat Nevin, Gary Stevens and John Aldridge, a redeveloped ground, and stable in the second tier. Just look at how far we've both come. Tranmere just relegated to League Two. And Burnley heading to the Premier League for the second time in six seasons.

We had reasons for optimism that day though. We'd just smashed our transfer record to bring in Kurt Nogan from Brighton & Hove Albion. A whopping £300,000, which was big money for us at the time. He was going to get the goals to keep us up. As it turned out, he didn't score that day at Prenton Park as we succumbed to a routine 2-0 defeat. He got a measly three goals that season as we were relegated, but an impressive 20 the next, by which point I was frequenting the same town centre pubs as him.

The boots belong to a lad called Michael Ihiekwe. I know this because his initials – MI – are on them. The unfortunate thing about that is that my initials are MH, so it looks like I've turned the H sideways on like this – H > I – in an attempt to be cool, or like I've come up with a logo for myself. I haven't. They're not my boots.

Saturday 21 June 2014

Bumping into somebody I've not seen for a while can be a bit awkward, mainly because they either don't know whether to say to me if they do know, or I don't know what to say to them if they don't know. And then sometimes I don't know whether they know or not, and if they do know they don't know whether I know that they know. Ouch.

And, nobody likes to say things out loud, especially not the word cancer. I don't mind it. It's very factual. It's reality. That's what Sean would say. And it's better than saying Big C.

So they say 'are you keeping well?' or similar, which doesn't really give you a clue either way. So you say 'aye yeah, not bad', which is just as vague. The usual line, though, which is used as proxy for 'I do know you have cancer' is 'you're looking really well'. Nobody used to say that to me before. Never. And now I'm getting it all the time – even though I'm as bald as Bobby Charlton. And let's face it, that alone makes me look like I've got cancer.

On the other end of the spectrum, though, you get the odd 'fucking hell, it's Duncan Goodhew'. Clearly, these types don't know and they think that I've either gone bald very quickly – some sort of world record – or I've done this by choice.

And at the wedding I'm at tonight, that is precisely what a lad called Phil has just said to me. Following the Goodhew comment the conversation goes something like this:

Phil: 'So, how you keeping?'

Now, because of the Goodhew comment, I know he doesn't know.

Me: 'Well, yeah, alright … do you know about this?' I'm pointing at my head.

Phil: 'What? You've had your hair cut?'

So I explain it to him, that it wasn't optional (what did he think I did, went to the barbers and asked for a 'refugee' cut), and that I'd been diagnosed with cancer and was having chemotherapy which had made my hair drop out.

Phil is shocked and replies with a variety of 'fucks, fucking hell, fuck me I'm sorry'. And then he says this:

'My dad always says to me, if he ever has to have chemo, I should just kill him.'

Hmmm. Strange thing to say to someone who's just told you he's got cancer and is having chemo.

I'm stunned that he's said this and explain (and I should know) that it's been grand. No problem at all. But Phil is adamant – his dad knows, chemo is worse than death and you're better off dead than having that.

'Phil, I'm having a great time,' I tell him as I drain another Brahma. 'I haven't had to go to work for three months, the sun's shining, the birds are singing, I've just been promoted, and there's a World Cup on telly.'

But he's not having it. He, his dad, and loads of others have already decided. Cancer/chemo, whatever, is a death sentence.

I know different. That it's not always the case. Not by a mile.

The weather is warm and the beer is cold and sweet. I just have to get it to the back of my neck. Quickly. I'm breaching my 14 units a week target. In a big way. I then move on and do the natural thing that I like to do at weddings – try to find any discarded half/partially full bottles of wine from the tables. These bottles have been abandoned and need a loving home. So I find a couple of friends and wander around swigging from the bottle. And when I can't find any more red, I move to white. And when there's no more bottles, I look for half-full glasses, of red, of white, of anything.

Sunday 22 June 2014

My wife greets me in the morning with 'you're cleaning that bathroom'.

I don't know what she means. I don't remember getting home.

The bathroom looks like somebody has spilled sangria in the sink, the toilet, on the floor, and walls and skirting board. But they haven't. Nobody was drinking sangria. It isn't sangria. It's red wine tinged puke.

I'm hungover for the first time in ages. Beautiful.

Monday 23 June 2014

I'm doing my Irish Football Association Level One Coaching badge.

When I filled in the registration form, there was a box to explain any medical issues they should be aware of. I left it blank.

In the usual introduction at the start of the course they ask to be made aware of any medical issues. By this stage I'd be daft to mention it. Not just because there's a chance they'd stop me doing the course. Even if they were happy to let me continue, they would, quite naturally, treat me a bit different, suggest I don't get involved in practicals, and assess me more leniently. I don't fancy that. It's quite nice to be somewhere with 50 fellow attendees and six coaches, and for none of them to have any idea about my 'disease'. There's no point in ruining that.

The course is brilliant. A massive amount of practical learning on the training pitch with loads of chances to get involved, which I do at virtually every opportunity. It is knackering, but brilliant all the same. I'm playing football all day instead of being in work. I am literally steaming by the end of the first day. I've not even had a drink.

Tuesday 24 June 2014
Costa Rica v England

Some of the course content is quite dry – in particular, today's two-hour first aid course and three-hour child protection course.

One of the great things about doing something like this though is the diversity. A lot of organisations use the word 'diversity', claiming that their staff are diverse and that's what makes them a great place to work. Frankly, that's nonsense. Different skin colours and ethnic origin does not equal diversity.

This, though, is real diversity. The age range for a start goes from 16 right through to 50+. But the background and the day jobs of the course attendees is wide ranging – students, ex-soldiers, tax accountant(s) (probably just the one), butcher, baker, and candlestick maker type thing. Plus, we even have one mixed-race lad which, in Northern Ireland terms, is the epitome of diversity.

Anyway, when you're used to spending your day with fellow tax accountants, spending time around other people who aren't tax accountants is pretty entertaining. You hear things that you wouldn't normally.

So, on the child protection, there are a few moans and groans about spending three hours on this when we would rather be playing football. I understand this completely, especially as what is right and wrong in relation to child protection is probably pretty obvious. So, one lad says to me:

'Three hours on child protection, what they going to be saying for three hours, it's simple isn't it? "Don't inappropriately touch any kids", what more is there to say?'

Later, there's a group of maybe 15 of us doing the child protection session. At the beginning the tutor asks whether anyone is coaching yet, and, if so, what age groups, to help him contextualise the session.

A few people start answering:

'Under 12s.'

'Under 8s.'

'Under 17s.'

Then one lad says:

'Me and Brian are doing an under-13s team.'

To which another lad sniggers and retorts:

'That came out a bit wrong.'

Like I say, tax accountants they aren't.

Other results mean that England are already out of the World Cup so the game against Costa Rica means nothing. I have a few Brahmas. It finishes 0-0. England have been dreadful compared to the brilliance of Burnley. It didn't used to be like that. It used to be the other way around.

Back in the summer of 1996, Burnley had just finished a disappointing season back in Division Two (third tier). We'd chanted 'sack the board' and 'Teasdale out' (sorry Frank!), and Jimmy Mullen had left the club and was replaced by Adrian Heath. And we hadn't won promotion back to Division One.

It was, at the time, the worst season I'd had watching the Clarets. It was expectations. That was it. For once, they were raised.

I'd just finished fourth year at secondary school. Fozzy had been right. I'd walked into the team at St Ted's and been ever present for four years. We got to the Keighley Cup Final no problem. Unfortunately, for the first time in years Burnley FC had decided they wouldn't allow the Turf to be used for the match. And, having won the cup for the last three years on the spin, we got hammered in the prestigious one. I felt a bit despondent towards football.

During the summer, England made up for it. England is a weird one. The country is too big, there are too many factions within it, and too much cultural diversity. We don't have the intimacy of the Welsh, Scottish or Northern Irish. I always want England to win, but like everybody else I'm too quick to knock them. They're not really mine. We're not that close. I've a tiny drop of Prussian in me, a good bit of Irish, but I'm mainly English. But I'm more Burnley, by a mile. I'm sure Jamie Carragher once said something similar about his (and fellow Scousers') devotion to Liverpool ahead of England. My nanna identified as much with Ireland as she did England, but had this crazy patriotism for the county of Lancashire. I think she wanted to liberate us from the rest of England.

That year, 1996, England timed it to perfection, just when Burnley weren't at it. Bang. Football came home. The only match I made it to was Italy against Germany at Old Trafford. It finished 0-0. And it was shite. But that can happen for the games that look good on paper.

I was 14, nearly 15. I'd even starting growing. I was getting into pubs (courtesy of a fake ID) and drinking Carling Black Label as though I liked it (and Hooch and Two Dogs when nobody was looking). Drinking wasn't just for getting drunk. It was compulsory, a social necessity. I have to thank alcohol. It pushed me on socially. I was bloody good at it.

The England boys got pissed up in Hong Kong before the tournament. They got a bit of stick in the media, but after we'd beaten the Scots 2-1 in the second group game it didn't matter. Gazza, one of the main protagonists from the Hong Kong incident, scored a belter and celebrated with the famous 'dentist's chair'. The whole thing only served to reinforce my views on drinking. I wanted to get pissed up on stuff like tequila, just like those boys. I wanted that bleached-blond hair as well. So I did both.

The 4-1 victory over the Dutch was probably the best I've ever seen England. Emphatic against quality opposition.

The quarter-final against Spain was a tough game. Spain were probably the better team but it was 0-0 at full time and still at the end of extra time. England won the shoot-out that followed, with Stuart Pearce (1990 victim against West Germany) burying his penalty. Well done Pyscho. We all felt those demons being exorcised. I watched that game in my mate's house near to Turf Moor. At full time we stumbled out on to the terraced streets, waving our England flags, which we'd probably got free with *The Sun* newspaper, and still drinking cans of Carling. We weren't alone. It was like an impromptu street party. 'It's coming home' bellowing out of everybody with a voice. It felt like a proper display of English patriotism. A rare showing of it.

Friday 27 June 2014

I go into work for a few hours. I don't do any work. I skim my emails, read the ones I need to read, and mark as read the ones that I can't be arsed to read. I have a coffee or two, wander about a bit and have a few chats. I've got used to not being here.

They always ask me how I'm feeling and whether I'm having any side effects. I must admit I'm struggling to think of anything. It's like I'm clutching at straws.

For the first few days after chemo my taste is a bit different. Some lagers taste very sweet, too sweet. But bitters are okay. That's good advice for somebody starting chemo – make sure you drink bitter for the first few days after treatment.

Certain McDonald's food is also sweeter. I eat that much of it I can tell. In particular, the sauce on a Big Mac is much, much sweeter, so much so that I'm occasionally going for a Big Tasty instead. The barbecue sauce is sweeter too. But let's face it, if these are my biggest issues I think I'm doing okay.

I'd heard about tiredness being a common problem. I have that sleepless night normally on the Tuesday after treatment (not the Monday) which is caused by the steroids, which leaves me a bit knackered on the Wednesday. But other than that I'm feeling as fresh as a daisy. It makes sense. Work for ten years in a job, which, whilst well paid, is pretty damn boring and time consuming, and then from nowhere get six months off at full pay. I'm alive and wide awake.

Another one I'd read about was the so-called 'chemo brain'. It's hard to tell with this one. When you're off work for that long you're bound to feel a bit less sharp mentally. After all, I spend most of my days drinking tea/watching SSN/doing a DIY job, and I have very little conversation. I find myself struggling to think of the odd word more often than I used to, even if it's something straightforward. And when you walk into a room and then forget what you were there for – yes, a bit more of that.

I find myself occasionally jumbling up a saying/sentence with another one. So, during a low-key domestic argument with the missus (and having cancer doesn't get you out of them!) I muddled up 'keep your hair on' with 'don't get your knickers in a twist' and shouted at her 'keep your knickers on'. I know, mental.

Having said that, I've done that before many times. I remember once speaking to a client on the phone and when he asked me how I was, I mixed up 'yeah, I'm well' with 'yeah, I'm not bad' and told him 'yeah, I'm not well'. It got a bit worse because he then asked what was wrong with me, and rather than correct my mistake I carried it on and told him 'yeah, I just keep being sick and all that, yeah'. I did get some strange looks from work colleagues sat around me, to whom this was complete news. These open plan offices. Crap.

I tell a few people about my football coaching course. I enjoy telling them, it provides a bit of spark, varies the conversation and drags it away from the normal cancer direction. They think I'm insane.

I think it's the sanest thing I've done in years.

Monday 30 June 2014
Me v Chemo Five

I'm back at the hospital for chemo number five – I'm on the home straight now. Three weeks today and it will be chemo number six and I will be done. For good, I hope. It's going slower than usual, and despite arriving at 8.30am, it's not until 10.30am that they tell me they won't be able to treat me today.

Apparently, my blood isn't right. No, they're not being discriminatory against Burnley Prussians. My bloods, per the lab analysis this morning, are sub-standard. Specifically, the neut count, which is a sub-set of the white blood cell count (the infection fighting cells), is too low. There is a threshold for your neut count, below which they won't give chemo to you (i.e. on the basis that the chemo will further batter the neuts and you'll end up with no immune system, which is, I presume, dangerous). The threshold is 1.0. They have all my scores on a computer system. At chemo number one my neuts score was 6.5. Today it's down to 0.73. That does sound a bit shit. The doctor tells me to come back in a week and it should have bounced back.

It's a bit frustrating, but would be a lot worse if I felt ill, or if my scan hadn't been clear. When I had the tumour on my neck I was keen as mustard to get each chemo done and dusted to get rid of it. But now that I've won anyway, as far as I'm concerned, whilst I still want it ticked off, I'm not quite as desperate. It's more the hassle of telling people that I haven't had treatment. They'll think I'm ill and I'll need to explain that I'm not and it's just this white blood cell technicality thing.

It's the 12-year-old-looking doctor today, so obviously I don't have too much faith in him (I'd have more faith in the guy bringing round the tea and biscuits). I'd heard before about injections you can have that boost the neut count so ask him whether I should have this. He says that it won't be necessary as it will be back up in a week's time. I go with it – you've got to trust them, haven't you?

I do a bit of googling on this neuts thing. I read on some American site that below 1.0 means no chemo (that bit is consistent with today) and below 0.5 is immediate hospitalisation. Blimey, I'm not too far away from 0.5. Americans, though, they're proper hypochondriacs, aren't they? Or maybe it's just the private medical companies creaming the medical insurance money?

Monday 7 July 2014
Me v Chemo Five (replay)

Groundhog Day – I'm back to the hospital for chemo number five. It's the usual thing, getting bored with it now. My bloods are done (much quicker this time) and then as usual I'm called in to see the doctor on duty. This time it's Dr Alshoufi. He's very odd and foreign but I do quite like him – he makes me laugh – I'm not sure if intentionally but I find him a source of amusement all the same – you have to find something to make you smile. He asks me how I'm feeling, and I tell him that, as ever, I'm feeling grand. He probes me a bit more and lists some of the standard questions – any headaches, temperatures, sickness etc.? I tell him no again.

'Unfortunately we can't treat you today,' he tells me, 'the neuts is still too low.'

He explains that it is very, very low – 0.17. So it is still falling, not bouncing back. I want to bounce back. It's a good job I'm not in America; they'd be putting me down with a score as low as that.

Now I'm a tiny bit annoyed. I've no idea why they didn't give me the booster injections last week. I take comfort in the fact that I was right and the 12-year-old was wrong. And also, in the grand scheme of things, it doesn't matter really. Like, it doesn't matter at all. At the back of my mind I'm thinking about a wedding I'm going to in mid-August. Ideally, I'd like a few weeks' gap between chemo number six and the wedding (given all the juice I'm going to drink), and any more delays and I could be compromising that. The reality is, though, if my biggest concern is ensuring that my alcohol appetite and fitness is in tip-top form for a wedding, then really I have no worries.

He says he will phone Dr Ong. Ah, we've not heard from her for a while. Dr Alshoufi dials the extension and speaks to the person on the other end. Wrong number. He scratches around his desk lifting scraps of paper trying to find her number, giving me the impression that he's never phoned her before, ever. He finds it, and tries again. Now he has her. I can hear him but not her. He tells her about the 0.17 score and then something like this.

'Yeah, it is very low.'

'Very low, yes.'

'No, he says that he feels fine.'

'No, nothing at all.'

'Well yes, he looks well.'

'Yes, obs all okay.'

He then starts scribbling some stuff down. He finishes the call with Dr Ong and lets me in on the plan.

'Okay, Dr Ong has recommended that you have a series of injections to boost your neuts count, and then come back this Friday for treatment.'

Really doc, you shock me.

The 'cunning plan' is that I have one injection on Monday, Tuesday, Wednesday and Thursday this week. If it works, that should boost the neut count for the chemo on Friday. They give me the first injection there and then and talk about arranging for a district nurse to come out to my house on Tuesday, Wednesday and Thursday. Sod that for a game of soldiers, I think – I'll do it myself.

Tuesday 8 July 2014

I wake up in agony. My back sort of feels sick. It's pain but something subtle, and at the same time agonising. It doesn't feel muscular. It's as though my back has a headache or is going to vomit. I'm no medic but I don't even need google to tell me that's not possible. It's my arms and legs as well – not as bad as my back but just achy. It's like all my limbs have given up on me.

We take the kids out to W5 (a kids' museum type place). After an hour or so I can barely stay on my feet. I need a chair. What is wrong with me? Is this it? The beginning of the end?

A bit like December 2001.

We'd been building for years under Stan Ternent; he kept us in Division Two in his first season, got us promoted to

Division One in his second season, and then we'd finished a respectable seventh in Division One the season after that.

By December 2001 we were halfway through the 2001/02 season and flying high at the top of Division One. We went to Maine Road on 29 December 2001, full of optimism, to play Kevin Keegan's Man City. By half-time we were 4-0 down after Paulo Wanchope had struck a hat-trick. It finished 5-1.

To make it worse, I was sat in the corporate seats in the rebuilt (1995) Kippax stand. I had to listen to City fans shouting 'come on, attack them, they're shit' every time they got the ball in our half. Sadly, I was starting to agree as City looked like scoring every time the ball was past the halfway line.

We didn't know it at the time but that defeat was the beginning of the end, not just for that season's promotion push as we slumped to seventh, but on Stan Ternent's time at Burnley. Two seasons of mediocrity followed and Stan left the club at the end of 2003/04. I did love Stan though, he got me through my exams at uni.

Incidentally, the handsome rebuilt Kippax, including its corporate boxes, lasted only eight years, as City left Maine Road in 2003 to move into a spaceship in East Manchester.

My new 3pm ritual takes my mind off my back for a few minutes. I depart to my study, lift up my top, grab a roll of fat from my stomach (there's no shortage of it) and shove a needle in. All good fun in many ways. I have to admit there is a real novelty value to this type of thing – it's a bit like when the supermarkets started those salad bars where you get a plastic container and fill it up with overpriced beetroot. You've got to make the most out of the novelty when you get some come your way.

I am surprised that I'm able to inject myself. Mainly because I thought it would be harder to do. They spent all of about 30 seconds showing me. The key thing here is that I'm not aiming this stuff (I wonder what's in it, kryptonite or something?) into a vein or anywhere specific. It's only a case of getting it in, anywhere will do. Bang. Done. The needle bit I've no issue with, even before this cancer lark I completely couldn't give two fucks about stuff like that. You've just got to do it. Take the medicine. Plus, any medical needle is a lot narrower and less painful than, say, a compass or a dart. Any lad with an older brother would say the same. I wonder if kids still need to buy compasses for school? And what about protractors? They were useful for the penalty area and centre circle if you were drawing a football pitch, but not much else.

As for needles, I've had more needles in me than a Scottish junkie, and enough blood taken from me to start a black pudding factory. Plus, the alternative would be for this chemo/cancer thing to absorb all five days of my week when two is more than plenty. The thought of having to wait around for a nurse to call three days in a row was incentive enough to stab myself. Even if I was home when she came I could be busy barbecuing.

Thursday 10 July 2014

The back pain is becoming pretty unbearable. What is happening to me? Maybe it was naïve of me to think I could get away with this. Finally, after four rounds of treatment, this chemotherapy is finally getting to me. Hands up chemo, you've really got me now.

At about 4pm I'm laid flat out on the sofa watching Major League Baseball highlights on the tele (as you do). My mind wanders and comes up with a hypothesis. Which is, 'is there a connection between the back pain and these injections?'

The timings coincide. I started the injections on Monday afternoon, and by Tuesday morning I could barely walk.

I manage to pull myself up off the sofa and rummage through the bin to find the box for the last needle which I'd used only an hour ago. I unfold the white piece of paper with a million tiny words on it in about ten languages. I don't know what is read less, instructions like these or the Gideons' Bibles in hotel rooms? I've never been so keen to read one of these. If this is a normal side effect then I'm not dying. If this is unusual then I'm fucked. Now, where is the English version?

Get in! It's a common side effect. It's the injections after all.

For the avoidance of doubt, I hate baseball. I have no idea why I was watching it.

Friday 11 July 2014
Me v Chemo Five (Second replay)

Here we go again then, take three for chemo number five. I'm like a footballer banging the goals in pretty frequently and then they dry up. I hit a barren spell. I get stuck on ten goals for the season, and game after game and chance after chance I just can't get off that ten-goal mark. It's so frustrating. One of the nurses asks how I had got on with the injections. I tell her that doing the injection was grand but that I wasn't expecting the back pain.

'Oh, did we not tell you about that? Oh yeah, definitely, you'd need to take painkillers for that.'

Nice one. No you did not tell me about that. I thought that my body was finally giving in. Here comes the slippery slope. You've run a good race lad and given it your best shot, hard lines. I thought it was time to bring the fucking bed downstairs.

Next up, Barbara, the cancer doctor, asks me the same question and I mention the unexpected back pain.

'That's fantastic,' she says.

What? What planet is she on? How can it be 'fantastic'? A pain in the arse side effect? Yes, I can believe that. Fantastic? Is she sick?

'Is it?' I offer.

'Yes, that's your bone marrow working hard. Your white blood cells will be up.'

'Ah.'

Now it all starts to make sense. Even though I still have no clue what bone marrow is.

And she's right. My white blood cells are up, and, importantly, the neuts have bounced back like the biggest bouncer backers ever, from 0.17 to a whopping 7.0. I don't really know what these numbers mean but it's improved more than 40-fold. Medicine, bloody marvellous stuff. I get the green light for the treatment to go ahead. Come on!

But today there is a different type of problem.

There's some old fella sat in my chair. My green chair in the corner. What the hell does he think he's doing? Can you believe it? Who the fuck does he think he is? I take the seat next to him, hoping that if he's left before I'm hooked up for the rituximab I'll take the chair back.

He's called Fred. And he's a right miserable sod.

The first time I hear him speak is when one of the nurses goes over, all friendly and smiley and nicey, and the best thing he's looked at this year, and she says, 'And how are you today Fred?'

One-word answer from Fred: 'Dreadful.'

Oh come on Fred, you miserable old git, that can't be it? Can't you just tell her that you're grand, or that you're hanging in there, or even ask her how she is. Ask her how she manages to motivate herself to deal with arseholes people like you? Oh no. Not Fred.

She then tells him that he'll get called in to see the doctor shortly.

'I don't like that doctor,' says Fred.

Well Fred, that's just tough shit.

A chap a couple of seats to my right is in much better form than Fred. I don't catch his name so we'll just say that he is called Ted. He's on his mobile phone all morning. At first I think he's planning a walk over the weekend with some friends (good on you Ted, that's the spirit), or maybe a sponsored walk or something. It seems to be requiring a lot of organising.

It then occurs to me that tomorrow is 12 July – the Battle of the Boyne – Ted's an Orangeman doing some organising for the march tomorrow. He's having some sort of blood transfusion whilst he's on the phone sorting all this out. I admire Ted's dedication.

They bring the dreaded 'lunch' out and I start to shiver. The stench of that soup. The nicey nurse who was talking to Fred approaches me. I've not met her before today. Her name badge says Eilíse which she tells me is pronounced like EYELASH. Strange that, you would think it would be pronounced like Eilíse, but apparently not. I let Eilíse down gently, revealing to her that, actually, I'm not a massive fan of the soup. She visually grimaces as I mention the word 'soup'. She agrees with me. I've always worried that when I decline the soup they think I'm being a bit of a snob about it, and that they might talk about me behind my back between themselves and refer to me as 'that English prick that won't take the soup'.

'It looks like vegetable today, that's not too bad,' says Eilíse. 'Wednesday is worst. It's always pea soup, and that's bowel cancer day. It goes right through them.'

Oh Eilíse, this is amazing – I thought it was just me.

This is great. I'm having soup banter here. Oh Eilíse, I think I love you.

I'm wondering whether I should maybe just take some of the cheese and wheaten bread that's on offer, when I hear Ted calling for help.

Oh dear, I hope he's okay. Turns out that he is, but his cheese isn't. It's blue apparently. Clearly, old Ted isn't a fan of blue cheese and is a cheddar man only. Fair dos, nothing wrong with that. A lot of the old timers round here won't drink Colombian coffee so there's no shame in not liking blue cheese. Personally, I'm not a massive fan either, but can do a bit of stilton provided that it comes with lashings of red wine, which, in fairness, is unlikely to be on offer today.

But oh no, I'm wrong. It's not blue cheese, it's cheddar that's gone blue. It's off. Rank. I'll hold out for a McDonalds when I get finished up then.

I've never done this on a Friday. So, as well as Eilíse, there's a few other nurses who I don't recognise. One of them does the name and address thing with me. As soon as I open my mouth she bursts out laughing.

'I was expecting something more exotic than that,' she explains herself.

Burnley is exotic! I know what she means though. I'm carrying a Prussian (exactly, what and where is that?) surname but I'm only one thirty-second Prussian, courtesy of some bloke, who, for reasons I don't know, left his house in Prussia and rocked up in Leeds during the 1840s. Shortly after that, he had a vision that later that century there would be an English Football League starting which would exclude Yorkshire in its entirety. He listened to his vision, drank and shagged as much as he could (easy enough because most of the locals went straight from the pub to the moors) and then ran off to the right side of the Pennines.

I provide the nurse with a version of this historical record, which is enough to satisfy her interest in my heritage.

I get home after my Big Mac meal and see that the Criminal Records Bureau check done via the Irish FA has come back in the post. Nothing on my record. I feel yet more weight falling off the shoulders. I'm relieved. Why? Well ... I feared there might have been ... I don't know how long these things last for ...

Way back in 2005 Burnley were drawn against Blackburn Rovers in the fourth round of the FA Cup. We'd barely played them in the previous 20 years so it's understandable that young men can get a little excited. There was a nightclub in Burnley Wood called the Circ (short for Circulation) which I had heard a lot about during my teens – it had a reputation for being a complete dive – but I had never been in. Until the day of the Blackburn cup game. It was a bit like being inside a cave, and that was not purely due to the decor and the fact there was no daylight. The clientele did their best too, which on that occasion included me, an excited young man, drinking in the morning in a pub with no windows. The game, however, was a bit of an anti-climax. It finished 0-0 with the only highlight (or should I say lowlight, although possibly not considering) being when a Burnley fan ran on and squared up to Robbie Savage. He must have been excited too. Fair dos.

A replay it was then, and a trip to Ewood on Wednesday, 1 March 2005. I left work in Manchester around lunchtime, bombed it back down the M66 and got into the Big Window in Burnley town centre for around 2pm. I think, from memory, the plan was that we were getting the 'coach' from the Turf at around 4.30pm. This time, though, for whatever reason, there wasn't the same stringent conditions on coach travel – it wasn't compulsory – although none of us wanted to drive so coach it was. But the juice was going down far too well and we soon realised there was not a chance we were getting on a coach. Luckily, some fellow Clarets in the same pub had booked a minibus with a local taxi firm. It turned out they had room for us and so we jumped in with them. Anyway, we'd no idea who these lads were but they were well up for it and popping pills of some variety as the driver took us down the M65 (and there was me feeling like a crafty devil for bringing my pint of Carling on board). It was probably around 5pm when we pulled up outside the Depot pub in Blackburn, on the canal bank, about two miles from Ewood.

There were a couple of coppers standing outside. It looked pretty low key. When we opened the door and walked inside it was a sight for sore eyes. The pub, a big one, was jam packed with Burnley fans, some of whom had clearly been there for hours. The singing was loud. It was electrifying. Zoo-like, but brilliant. What was happening in the toilets was what my three-year-old would call 'a bit like different' – the cubicles were full of lads doing coke off the seats (no need to shut the door, no room anyway, even if there is a copper only yards away), people were pissing in the sinks and the urinals were filling up with broken beer bottles. It was pure chaos. And I was buzzing. Only a few hours ago I'd been sitting at my desk, in an office, doing tax accounts. Now here I was, in the Depot pub, in Blackburn, on their manor!

We bumped into a lad from school a few years older than me who had nipped out to the local Tesco, and returned, via the canal entrance at the back, with a litre of Smirnoff vodka. I realised that loads of them were doing this. Now, it's difficult to hide a full litre in your coat pocket, and he was happy to offload what he could. I held out my half full pint of Stella and he filled it up to the top. Shortly after that, the police (now in much larger numbers) stormed in and forced the landlord to close the pub for the day. I emptied my glass down my neck. We left the pub.

The scene outside was a shock. Once in the car park, the Burnley fans (a group of us around 200 strong) were penned in by a line of police of a similar number. There were numerous vans dotted around, dozens of dogs and a helicopter overhead. As the police 'escorted' us to the ground (the long way, avoiding the town centre) I saw a number of lads getting arrested and thrown into vans – some were trying to break free from the escort, others walking around the periphery just seemed to be getting picked off at random. But it felt amazing, like I was a Burnley warrior walking into battle, arms outstretched above my head, bellowing out 'No Nay Never' like a demented drunk Scotsman on a day out at Wembley. I stayed at the front of the group, in the centre. Our Jim tapped me on the shoulder a couple of times and told me to hang back. I ignored him. He then jumped on me from behind and grabbed me in a bear hug. I threw my right elbow back into him in the general direction of his ribs and told him to fuck off. Within seconds I was on the floor, and could see fluorescent yellow from the corner of my eye. Unfamiliar voices. Scousers. A cord was tied around my wrists. They threw me in the back of a van.

As it turned out, it wasn't our Jim that had grabbed me, but a copper. A mate had seen four coppers pile on top of me and take me away. He asked one of them what I had been arrested for. Assaulting a police officer was the apparent answer.

The journey to wherever it was they were taking us was a long and painful one. There were only a handful of us in the van, and every now and then the van would stop, one of them would open the back door, get in, and ram a head against the wall of the van. Big brave lad.

I couldn't see it but I could feel my head. It was missing a lot of skin. When I got to the station the officer on the desk asked me how I had got my injuries. Well, interesting question is that, friend. I told him I didn't have any injuries. He asked again. All I said was that I didn't have any injuries when I got in the van.

My first time in a police cell. I was bored beyond belief, and quickly sobering up.

I had some fingerprints and photographs taken by a nice Irish policewoman in her 60s who believed everything I told her and was telling everybody that would listen that I had done nothing wrong and that I was a good boy.

I had no idea what time it was. I needed to be at a client site in Crewe by 9am and had arranged to meet a colleague in the office in Manchester at 7.30am. I was shitting myself – would I lose my job? Holy fuck, I hadn't meant for this to happen.

I got out about 1.30am. I was in the office before 7.30am.

As me and my colleague Charlie got in the lift to head out to see the client, we were met by one of the senior partners, a hard Scot called Jim. He glared at the lack of skin on my forehead and the bright red lava showing beneath where it had once been, and asked what I'd been up to.

'Playing five-a-side,' I said.

'Tough game,' he replied.

I don't know if he believed me.

Other colleagues who knew I'd been to the game got a different story. My version for them was that I had been at the game when a mysterious piece of wood came flying through the air and caught me on the head. They definitely didn't believe me (how many different pieces?) but still they didn't know the truth. And having watched clips of Micah Hyde's goal on the internet I raved about it as though I had been there. But anyway, I was in Crewe with the client by 9am churning out tax returns like a proper good boy accountant, whilst the hooligan inside me was quietly grinning at my double life.

And there is no trace of these events on a CRB check.

Friday 18 July 2014

I'm back in the office for a couple of hours just to show my face. I need to keep doing this. I think I'd feel like a bit of a dick being off for months and then coming back in 'da-da' to a grand entrance like a celebrity, as though I was wanting attention, and them all saying stuff like 'welcome back' or 'hello stranger'. It would be so embarrassing I'd rather just call in for a few hours every couple of weeks.

I'm chatting to a colleague who is asking me the standard questions.

'You say the same every time,' he tells me, 'have you actually been sick at all during this?'

'No, not once. I've never even felt sick.'

I'm still not sure. I'm hungry. I'm so hungry I feel sick. Or do I feel so sick I'm confusing it with hunger? It's a bit like flashing your hand under a tap for a split second and getting confused between hot and cold.

I do like food. And apart from watching Sky Sports News there isn't that much to do during the day midweek. So I am eating like a pregnant woman. The weather has been okay and I like meat, so I've been perfecting what I call the 'one-man BBQ'. Most days this involves visiting the local supermarket to buy some fresh meat. Some things are good value, chicken wings and pork ribs especially, and those giant turkey legs. I feel like a caveman eating those, they're great. Making some sort of marinade using various things from the cupboard is always a bit of craic, and then it would be wrong to rush the grilling.

The whole lunch 'experience' is taking me about three hours from start to finish, but you have to fill the day somehow, don't you.

Tuesday 24 July 2014

I'm worried that we haven't done enough business in the transfer market.

The problem with Sky Sports News and all the other media is that it's instantaneous. So you immediately know when you haven't signed anybody yet. Because, if you had, you'd have heard about it straight away from SSN, or some update or app or something.

It used to be so different. The first you might hear would be reading it in the *Burnley Express*, or more likely the *Lancashire Evening Telegraph* (it was daily), or on Radio Lancashire. Or you could waste 50p per minute calling Clubcall. But word of mouth, that was different. I hear nothing by word of mouth anymore. These days my phone has already told me everything.

We used to go to France during the summer for the first three weeks of July. It was prime time for transfers. So every afternoon, at about 5pm (because we knew the *Lancashire Evening Telegraph* would be out by then), me and our Jim crammed into a phone box to phone Grandad. It normally cost about five francs, or, if we had done the business and there was more to talk about, as much as ten.

I remember punching the number in:
0044128225776

Exactly, who remembers phone numbers these days? Apart from stalkers.

We'd get the lowdown, based on everything he was hearing. From the newspapers, the radio, the papershop talk, Rosegrove Unity, Burnley Cricket Club. We always expected/wanted big news, but we normally came out of the phone box feeling short-changed. But that anticipation, the not knowing, we might have, we might not have signed someone. We just didn't know.

That day in 1994, when Grandad told us we'd smashed our transfer record to sign Liam Robinson from Bristol City for £250,000, we came out of the phone box on cloud nine. We probably drank a shitload of Kronenburg to celebrate – from a young age I did a lot of my training on those 250ml bottles. Robinson flopped at Burnley. He managed nine league goals in 63 appearances before moving on to Scarborough.

Thursday 26 July 2014

I have too many trees in my garden, about 25 of them, all 30 to 40 feet high. I thought it was a good idea to get somebody in to take 10–15ft off the lot. I also thought it was a good idea to tell them to leave all the wood for me.

It wasn't. Because I'm staring at the biggest mound of garden waste I've ever seen. Foliage, leaves and branches, about 5ft high, and covering an area of about 20ft squared.

It's my fault, brought about by a combination of trying to knock a few quid off the price, but mainly to give me something to do.

But not this much to do.

Gardening was another thing Dr Ong told me not to bother with. Too much risk of bacteria and given my lower immunity etc., etc. Having said that, this task ahead of me isn't so much gardening, it's a waste management contract.

If you want to finish you have to start. I fold the seats down in the car to maximise the space.

I start by stuffing as much of it as I can into bin bags. It's a disaster. The bags are too small and they're ripping up. Thankfully my neighbour is laughing at me over the garden fence, and throws over a few builders' merchant-type sacks. These are just the ticket. It takes me about ten minutes to produce four cubes of waste, which consumes most of the room in the car.

The only problem now is when I look at the garden it looks like I haven't moved anything. Because, relatively, I haven't.

I get in the car and make the short journey to the recycling centre.

The first load takes more than an hour from start to finish, but I soon find a rhythm where the whole 'cycle' is down to about 30 minutes. It's a bit like rituximab, but different.

When you drive into the recycling centre you stop at the barrier, tell the chap what type of waste you have, and he directs you to a free bay. I'm surprised when on my fifth trip down the same bloke at the barrier is still asking me 'What you got, mate?'

I mean, he can see in the car, the seats are down, and it's ram jam packed with garden waste, plus he's asked me the same question and I've given him the same answer four times in the last couple of hours. It's like I'm talking to a machine. He's on auto pilot.

By the time I make my 14th and final trip, seven hours after the first, and he's still asking, I start to think he's taking the piss. By this stage I've abandoned the hope of keeping the car remotely clean, I'm lobbing as much crap in as I can, it's piled high on the passenger seat, and I've got leaves and twigs coming out of my ears. I look like Worzel fucking Gummidge.

I get home and admire the now empty spot. But there's a tree that's bugging me. Only about 12 to 15 feet tall, wispy, planted right in the middle of the garden. It does my head in. I've never liked it. Fuck it, I'm taking you down. I head to the garage, find a woodsaw, say hello to the previously shit-stained boxer shorts which are dry and can now be brought back into service but I put them in the bin anyway, and return to the tree.

I pick a spot, two or three feet up, and start to attack it. It's only about five inches in diameter but it's heavy going with just the woodsaw. It's a good ten minutes of hard labour before I bring it down. That just leaves the stump to remove. I've a couple of feet to play with as leverage. It's a bit like fighting a dwarf. I knock ten bells out of him. This way and that. I feel the ground loosening up around the base but he still won't go down. I take a mallet to him and beat him senseless. After about 20 minutes of venomous attack he finally buckles. Good. I'm completely knackered.

My shirt is soaked and has long since been discarded. I lie down, next to the tree. My victim. I'll have a beer.

I nip inside for a Coors Light and return to my fallen friend. The great thing about Coors Light is that I feel healthy drinking it. It's on a par with a probiotic yoghurt I think, although I've never had one of those.

I savour the moment. It's been an enjoying and rewarding day – eight hours of pure hard graft. It was all completely pointless and unnecessary, but I enjoyed it.

Monday 28 July 2014

Finally a breakthrough. I take a phone call from a bloke at Ards FC Academy. He wants to know if I'm still interested in coaching. Hallelujah. I thought they had forgotten all about me. I've been privately swearing about this lot. Yes, of course I'm still interested.

He asks me to come down to the first training session of the season. It's on Wednesday night. Two days away.

Football, it's beautiful. Bring me down one minute; lift me back up in the next. I can think of so many examples of that.

Burnley had finished sixth in the Second Division in 1993/94 and took the final play-off spot. We were 12 points behind third-placed Plymouth, who we were playing in the semi-final. We really didn't have a right to be promoted, and didn't expect to be, especially not after we'd only managed a 0-0 draw at home in the first leg of the semi, with the young Plymouth keeper Alan Nicholls in fine form.

I remember the night of the second leg at Home Park very well. I was always football. But at school I dabbled in other things like cross-country running and athletics, which were independent of football and never caused any sort of clash. I'd recently played tennis a few times at school during PE lessons, and, because nobody in Burnley plays tennis and I had played before (mainly on holiday), I was above average. I must have been one of the best, in fact, because that Wednesday night I was asked to play in a tennis match for the school. Now, I didn't even know schools did tennis matches, certainly not my school, but I was flattered to be one of only four boys asked to play. Don't get me wrong, I was no Pete Sampras, but in 1994 I was top four in the second year at St Ted's in Burnley.

The problem was, I had a cup final that night for my football club, and I wouldn't be able to make it to both. Sounds like a no-brainer? Has to be the football? It wasn't though. It hadn't been going great at my new team AC Inter.

The team were great, they were winning everything. But I was barely getting a look in. It was the choice between the novelty of a tennis match or potentially playing just a few minutes in a cup final.

Of course, I'm football. It had to be football.

I was an unused sub. I felt like a fraud winning a cup final and collecting a medal that I hadn't really won.

And I felt like shit in that dressing room taking off an unused kit. Until, that is, word made its way in, surely via a car or portable radio (no smartphones in those days) that Burnley were 2-1 up at Plymouth. I was stunned that we were winning. I hadn't thought we had a chance. And we'd scored twice. Football. Kill me one minute; bring me back to life in the next.

We listened to the game on Radio Lancashire on the way home and I was dancing around the kitchen when I heard the third goal had gone in. My dad landed home with my brother, whom he'd just collected from his football training a few minutes later, and was having hard words with him. Apparently, as they were driving home my brother celebrated the third goal in a bit of a weird way by taking off his seat belt and jumping on to the floor of the car, as you do. The full-time whistle went shortly after that and we were a happy house. We were going to Wembley. And my nightmare 'match' from earlier that evening was long forgotten.

I was never asked to play tennis ever again. Federer and co must have been mightily relieved.

The Plymouth keeper, Nicholls, despite being capped for England under-21s during the summer of 1994, was released at the start of 1995/96 following a tough time with injuries. He played a single game for Stalybridge Celtic of the Conference in November 1995, and sadly died in a motorcycle accident on his way back home from the match.

Wednesday 30 July 2014

I don't know how to prepare for this. What am I doing? Watching? Coaching? I don't know what to expect. And what age group? There is no briefing. But this is the real world. Real life. I'm outside of the Big Four bubble. What even is a briefing?

I read over the files I'd got from the Grassroots and Level One courses just to have some material in my head. Nevertheless, I am shitting myself.

I arrive at 6.15pm and there are already loads of kids there. A gazebo has been set up on the edge of the pitches. Forms are being filled in and kit tried on. The chap on the phone had mentioned something about registration. This must be that then. I look for a familiar face and I can't find one. I want to get back in the car and go home. I'm a grown man and I've turned up in football kit and blue boots. I probably look a bit dodgy.

I spot one of the committee members I'd met about a month ago and she catches me looking. Thank God. I tell her that I'm looking for Jon. Cue lots of shouting about the whereabouts of Jon. Several people are involved. Blimey, I've somehow caused quite a commotion.

Jon appears. I've definitely not met him before. As we walk across one of the pitches he tells me I'm the new manager of the 2007 age group. It doesn't feel like there is much room for negotiation on this. Nor time. The kids are about 50 yards away and we're walking towards them. And I've just been appointed as their manager. That gives me roughly 30 seconds to explain that I'm uncomfortable coaching this age group because of their proximity to George's age, and George is another son I have but he doesn't live with me he lives in England because I left his mum when she was pregnant, and so I want to resign. I've no chance. He introduces me to a few coaches. There's about five of them. I learn their names, then I forget them instantly because I'm still so nervous.

I get the gist that the 2006 and 2007 age groups have trained together in the past, but they're now splitting them, and I'll be managing the 2007s. There looks to be plenty of coaches to me but what do I know? I've told Jon that I've not coached before. He asks the 'leader' of the pack of coaches if we can keep the kids together tonight to ease me into it. He agrees.

There's a good number of kids, maybe 25. I've no idea which are 2006 and 2007. I'm told, but then I forget, they all seem to be the same and there are too many. Just like the names. There's too many.

They learn mine though and I start to hear it a lot. I'm taken aback though when one of them says, 'Michael, you've got the same boots as me.'

I stare at the seven-year-old's feet. His boots are hideous. They're blue ... and orange ... and yes, the same as mine. Oh dear.

The leader-of-the-pack coach is really impressive. I'm wondering whether he has his A licence or maybe even Pro so I'm surprised when he tells me he only has Level One. On paper I'm as qualified as him. That's clearly bollocks.

It's nice to be outside. On grass. The smell of it – freshly cut – is gorgeous. Smells of summer. With footballs. It's noisy. It's full of life. A million miles away from the McDermott Unit.

He finishes the session with a penalty shootout and asks the kids which of the coaches they want to go in goal. A few of them say my name. I'm flattered. It's nice to be wanted. It's really nice. Soon a load of them start shouting MI-CHAEL! MI-CHAEL! I feel like I'm going to cry.

I adopt a strategy of try with the good strikes, don't try with the poorer ones, but don't blatantly let them in if they're really bad. It flies in. Bring on next week.

Monday 4 August 2014
Me v Chemo Six

A few weeks later than I'd planned, but all being well, this is my final treatment and I'll never see this place ever again. As in, I've a preference (a strong one I should add) not to have cancer again.

As far as the treatment goes, I can't really explain how indifferent I feel towards it. I don't dread it. I don't look forward to it. I just turn up. I sit in various chairs. And it's fine.

Whilst waiting for the bloods to come back from the lab, I chat to an old chap in the waiting room.

'It's a long day is this,' he sighs.

He's about 70-odd – most of them seem to be. I hear other patients repeating their birth dates to the nurses and the most common decades by birth are 1930s, 1940s then 1920s. I've never even heard anybody say 1950s, never mind 1980s. The implication of this is that I've never met a fellow patient younger than my own parents – they're all older. I guess that explains why, again, I'm the only one in shorts.

He's a nice chap. Chatty, positive, upbeat. He tells me his isn't curable, but can be managed. He might get another ten years (which he adds, at his age, will do him 'rightly'), and, whilst around 12 months ago he was having a tough time, at the moment he's finding the management of his cancer to be manageable.

We talk about the drugs and how amazing it is that they seem to work. I show him the picture of me on my Blackberry taken the morning before my first chemo.

'Oh yeah, you were a lot heavier then,' he says.

I'm only showing him a headshot. He's mistaken the tumour as some sort of neck fatness. It definitely wasn't a bollock by that stage. It was massive – over 20cm in length. For what it's worth, despite eating like I was in training for some sort of Man v Food competition, my weight has remained steady throughout my treatment.

He tells me that for the last three weeks since his last round he's done three weeks on a boat on the Norfolk broads with his kids and grandkids. Some of his grandkids are toddlers, similar age to my youngest two. God knows how I would get on on a boat with those two wee mad men – we'd be putting them to sleep with armbands on.

He's called in for his treatment so I watch daytime tele. It's bad, but not as bad as the choice of magazines in here – I open up a *Camping and Caravanning Monthly*. I don't take much from it, but at least I know never to buy it, if I was ever to be tempted. About 15 minutes later he comes back, and offers me his hand.

'You're all done?' I ask him.

'Yeah that's me, good luck for the rest of your treatment.'

Bloody hell, it's only 10.30am and he's away home. Long day this, isn't it? The day's not even started yet. Clearly he was a civil servant back in the day.

I get out at about 2pm, which has come to be about average (excluding chemo one). It isn't a long day, but it does feel like one. It really is a bit like going on a plane journey. There's lots of stopping and starting and general messing about before the plane takes off, then when it does take off you're stuck in a chair, wishing the time away. And for large parts of my treatment I have a drip attached to me, which means if I need to go to the toilet I need to take it with me. It's a bit of a pain in the arse.

You can use your phone (not like a plane) but there is no wi-fi. And the TVs are generally crap, like most planes.

And at the end of it all, when you get up, you feel a wee bit tired and that the legs need a stretch, even though you've been doing nothing.

Wednesday 6 August 2014

Two days after my last chemo I'm back out on the grass. This is the big one. Tonight we're splitting the groups so I'll be doing the coaching.

Coaching. Managing. A team of my own. Just like Dyche.

I pull up on the car park less nervous than last week but more nervous at the same time. I've met the people – they know who I am – I'm fine with that bit. It's the coaching bit that's now worrying me. The only coaching I've done was on the Level One course, where the people you're coaching are the fellow course participants. Adults. They do what they're told and have reasonable ability.

I've walked barely ten yards from the car when, seemingly from nowhere, Jon jumps out of the back of a van and throws a load of gear down beside me. He nods at me and points at it. He seems to be a man of few words but none were really needed so that's probably okay. I have a big bag of balls (there are loads of jokes you can make about ball bags), must be at least 20 size threes in there, a stack of cones and a long bag with poles in it.

Even though I don't have any Ards training kit yet, my attire does make me look the part. I'm wearing Wolves training gear that Carl sent me. A passer-by might even think it's mine, and that the CH initials are mine. As though I'm an ex-Wolves coach.

Leader-of-the-pack coach gets all the kids in and explains that they're splitting the group into 2006 and 2007s. He then identifies which kids are going with him (i.e. 2006) and which are with me (2007). I soon realise it's not quite that simple. Some of the 2007s are 2006 players. Eh? One in particular is not happy. 'I'm a 2006 player,' he protests.

'What year were you born?' Leader asks, knowing the answer.

'2007,' says the kid.

'Well you're a 2007 player.'

This leads to a mini tantrum. I can kind of feel for the kid. He's cherry-picked a couple of the higher-ability 2007 players to stay with the 2006 group. Up until that moment this kid probably thought he was one of the best 2007s – he's now getting 'feedback' in a roundabout way that he isn't.

The split leaves me with ten players, and the 2006s about 18–20.

I've learnt that the leader isn't the manager, he is a coach. So I know that at least those two are with the 2006s. There are another four coaches and I've no idea who they are.

As the 2006 kids drift off to another area of the pitch, I watch as, one by one, all the coaches go with them and I'm left on my own.

Hmmm. I wasn't expecting that. It's like something from an American film and I'm the lonely kid on the playground who has just moved to town because my dad has a new job or something like that.

Oh well. There goes my backroom team. I probably never had one.

There's a couple of parents (of the 2007 kids) stood watching the session (which hasn't yet started because I'm still looking bemused). I can feel them looking at me. I look back. They look as puzzled as I do.

Now for the coaching. The leader tells me as he walks off to just play a match if I want, to get a chance to see how good the kids are. I tell him that would be too easy. He likes my answer.

I set up a basic passing and receiving drill. One straight out of my Level One toolbox.

It's a complete disaster.

I stop one boy because he's blatantly, so I think, messing about. I tell him he has to pass the ball to the boy at the opposite cone. He taps the ball forward a few yards and then looks at me.

I say, 'no, you've got to pass it to him.' I throw the ball back to him. He attempts it again. I say attempt, because he is trying. He can't kick it that far. I've spaced these cones out way too much. I look at the other pairs of boys and they are equally making a right mess of this. It must look terrible on the eye. I hurriedly bring the cones in a bit. The passing gets slightly better, they can reach the distance at least. Some have no accuracy. The receiving at the other end is worse. I'll tell you what, fuck passing.

It gets better after that, we do some dribbling exercises, one on ones, and finish with a match. It probably looked okay in the end, maybe even looked as though I knew what I was doing.

By the time I've packed up the car with my new 'belongings' it's 8pm. I've not given a single thought to cancer for at least two hours. I haven't had time. It's such a fantastic distraction is this; I cannot lose focus even for a second and it's nerve-racking as hell, but so worth it. I've put a new stamp on myself tonight.

Friday 15 August 2014

So chemo six is all done and dusted, and I'm feeling grand still. It's been a doddle, this – a walk in the park, a stroll on the beach. So far.

I've made it to Eugene's wedding and I feel like having a few shandies. If only they were shandies though. I rarely drink shandy. Years ago, on a night out after work in Manchester I had offered to be the driver for the night for the few of us heading back to the metropolis (that's Burnley obviously). All was good – I resisted and stuck to shandy all night long. We set off home about 11ish, stopping for a moment at the bus stop on Deansgate to let in another Burnleyite after I'd spotted him waiting for the bus. When we got off the motorway at Rawstenstall I noticed a police car out of the rear-view mirror. Right behind me. He was still there at Crawshawbooth, at Dunnockshaw, at Clowbridge. Oh shit.

'Chaps, that copper has been behind me for miles now.'

'So? I thought you haven't been drinking?' asked Malcolm, the bus-stop passenger.

'Well, I've been on shandy,' I replied.

'How many you had?' asked Mal.

As I try to answer this I realised I wasn't on the cusp of being over the limit, I'd smashed it.

'Maybe … 12.'

'What, halves?'

'Err, no.'

'Oh fuck.'

Finally, at the summit junction, I indicated right, the copper went straight on. There are few things more stressful than feeling completely sober whilst clearly over the legal limit, all the while with a copper up your arse.

Back to the wedding, I start the day in a sensible frame of mind. The wedding is near Dungiven, and the reception is across the border in Letterkenny, so my friend and ex-work colleague David has agreed to drive. I'm well pleased as I don't fancy the prospect of the drive back the next day on the notorious Glenshane pass. It's a bit of a road trip for us, a couple of hours' drive. I want to bring beers for the journey but feel bad doing that in somebody else's car. Fortunately, my driver knows me only too well, as he's got a couple of chilled San Miguels waiting for me.

'I'm taking it easy,' is my motto at the reception. I repeat it all day long – pints only, no spirits, and slow pace, no necking. From 3.30pm to 1.30am when it ends I stick to this and probably only do a pint an hour (okay ten pints but over a very long period) – I feel sober but probably aren't – and feel like I could drink at this pace all day long. I even decline the odd glass of wine, which I have never done at a wedding. My normal policy is 'drink when offered'; it's the drinker's equivalent of a footballer's 'shoot on sight'.

A work colleague who I haven't seen for a few weeks is impressed with my returning hair. It's growing back consistently all over my head and is at about a number-two length. As he puts it, 'Your hair's looking good, because, fucking hell, that day I saw you in the office, God, I didn't want to say anything to you at the time, but, you looked fucking awful.' Cheers for that.

I'm just about to retire for the night when I'm drawn to the residents' bar. By that I mean drawn by the fact that it exists and is open. Go on then, I'll have a Jameson. One quickly turns to two, then three. Then the bar gets busier with other wedding guests. I run out of Euros but it doesn't seem to matter – the drinks are lining up in front of me, Guinness, Jameson, some shots that I've no idea about, and I'm gobbling it all up like a thirsty schoolboy on his first night out on the town.

Saturday 16 August 2014

I wake about 10am feeling slightly groggy but not too bad/ still a wee bit pissed. David asks me how long I was in the bar for. I don't actually remember but I recall asking the barman what time he was closing the bar for the night and he told me 4.30am.

'Not sure, sometime just after half four I think.'

I'm glad I'm not driving. David isn't. He's not up to it yet so we hang around in the hotel bar for a while. Soft drinks for him. Shandy for me.

The United–Swansea game kicks off on the tele and there's a few more people now watching with us, including plenty of guests from the wedding. One of the cousins (another, seems to be tons of them) approaches me.

'Late one last night then, eh?'

'I don't know, what time was it, half four ish?' I say.

'Well,' he replies, 'when I left at five to six there were only two people still in the bar.'

'Who?' I ask.

'Eugene [the groom] … and you.'

Oh well. These things happen.

I'm proud of my achievement. That's proper drinking. I'm back in the saddle. Welcome back big lad.

Monday 18 August 2014
Burnley v Chelsea

Back in the Premier League. Back on TV again. We're starting our season live on *Monday Night Football*. Brilliant if you live in Bangor; ballache if you live in Burnley.

Scott Arfield scores a screamer early on to put us into the lead and I start to think we're going to pull off a major shock.

Not for long though. Chelsea and Cesc Fabregas in particular are a different class and by the 34th minute we're 3-1 down. Chelsea take the foot of the gas in the second half and that's how it ends.

Not the romantic story I was hoping for. But I can't complain. It's Chelsea. I wasn't expecting anything more. Just hoping for it. Hope is good. I like hope.

Burnley had drawn Chelsea away in the third round of the League Cup in 2008/09. Not that we have ever cared that much about the League Cup, but when you've drawn Chelsea away it takes on a different complexion. It wasn't about winning, we knew we didn't have a chance of that, but the prospect of a day (well, night for a League Cup game) in the Big Smoke and the chance to visit a ground where I'd never seen Burnley play.

Our Jim had moved to Grand Cayman just a couple of weeks earlier and was gutted to miss it. Little old unfashionable Burnley taking on those Chelsea boys. Rich against poor. South against north. David against Goliath. Or even England v Russia. It was a mouth-watering prospect.

I got to London early and made sure I poured plenty of juice down my neck. It's a fantastic location is Stamford Bridge – a superb venue for pre-match drinking for the 6,000 Burnley fans who packed out the away end. It was a jovial atmosphere, largely because we were there for the occasion, and even Didier Drogba's goal just before the half-hour mark didn't dampen our spirits. And that was all pretty standard, and to be expected. We weren't out of the game, but we were getting beat. It was respectable. With half an hour to go, Coyle decided to bring on Ade Akinbiyi, shortly after which Chelsea made a substitution of their own, taking off the ever-dangerous Drogba.

One minute later the 6,000 of us went mental as, right in front of us, big Ade swept the ball in after Chris Eagles' shot was blocked. In an instant it all changed – there were only 20 minutes left and we weren't getting beat. We hadn't seen this coming.

We didn't threaten another goal, but saw out the remaining time and an additional 30 minutes of extra time, our only casualty being a late red card for Steven Caldwell. The penalty shoot-out was taken at the Chelsea end. I started to think we could do this. We had a chance. But no, surely not?

The big Dane Brian Jensen saved a couple of penalties and we had won, prompting utter disbelief and delirium in the away end all rolled into one. I looked at the line of stewards sat at the bottom of the stand, facing the crowd rather than the pitch, missing the action. I often feel for those guys, having to watch the crowd, but not that night. They had front-seat viewing for the best show in town – 6,000 Burnley fans celebrating a win at the Bridge.

A few more pints followed before I went back to my hotel room with my pick-up for the night. I was staying in an Easy Hotel; there wasn't enough room to swing a cat in, never mind eat a KFC. I ate fried chicken in the bathroom, before collapsing on the bed. London. Shithole.

Thursday 21 August 2014

'Do I really have to go in the wheelchair?' I ask the nurse for the second time.

A wheelchair, at my age. I feel like a right dick.

It's been two and a half weeks since my last chemo, five days since Eugene's wedding and I'm back in the cancer unit. In a fucking wheelchair.

I'd had an inoffensive cold for a couple of days and had been trying to deal with it by eating Lockets. I'd never read the blurb on a packet of Lockets but I do check – the only advice is that children under the age of seven shouldn't eat more than three packets in one day. But why on earth would they do that? The Lockets didn't work. I woke up this morning with aching limbs and a mouth drier than a Qatar World Cup. And hot. Too hot. I checked my temperature, and for the first time I'm over 37.5°C, I'm 38.0°C. As per my chemotherapy alert poster which has been up in the kitchen for the last five months not being looked at, this means I need to call the emergency number. I do, and they tell me to get up to A&E pronto. I've finished with all this shit, haven't I?

I don't quite do what she says. It's out of hours when I call but I know the McDermott Unit will be open soon enough so go straight there.

This is the benefit of being treated on the NHS. Had I had my chemo done privately, in an emergency like this I'd have no other choice than to go to A&E. Having been treated on the NHS though, I am able to go straight to the cancer centre and get seen by people I know. Really takes the stress out of it. I love the NHS.

I get there at 8.15am. They sit me down and take my temperature. It's still up, 38.4. They take bloods and put me on a penicillin drip. They warn me early on that I might need to be admitted for a few days.

The blue curtain is put up around my chair. This is a first – I've seen other people having this done and always wondered why they need the blue curtain – what goes on behind there? Are they dying? There's a doctor and three nurses (all female) sat around me.

They just talk. They clarify that if my neuts count is lower than 1.0 I will need to be admitted. I'm not hopeful, as I've had neuts scores of 0.17 and 0.73 (on the days when I was refused treatment) and I was feeling fine on those days.

I'm wearing shorts (it's my summer uniform – I haven't worn jeans during the day since May) and the back of my thighs are sticking to the chair. I don't feel too bad. Just like a normal cold, only hotter. The combination of penicillin and paracetamol starts to kick in and I feel my temperature coming down. When the nurse comes to check I tell her that it's coming down, and expect it to be 37.5 or below. She checks it – 37.7.

The blood test results come back from the lab – the nurse is smiling so it must be good. 'They're fine,' she says. 'Neuts are 16.'

16? I had 0.17 just a few weeks back. I wonder what the top score is for a neut count? I want to win it. I wonder if there's a prize. I think that's a personal best for me anyway.

A few minutes later my temp is below 37.5. All of a sudden it's looking good.

'We'll do the chest x-ray, and provided that's clear we'll monitor you for an hour or two, then you can go.'

My blood pressure is low so they insist I need a wheelchair to go to x-ray. I'm relieved now that it looks like they'll let me go home, and this will be my last-ever time in a wheelchair. I don't complain. The x-ray is clear and now I've just got one or two hours to sit through.

They offer me some magazines from the waiting room. No chance. I'll play on my phone. In fact, even if I didn't have a 3G signal I'd rather practise texting than open *Camping and Caravanning Monthly* again. I politely decline.

I get out of there at 11.30am with some take-home pills (more the merrier hey). Luckily I avoid lunch, and the smell of the soup. I've not eaten (save for three bourbon creams at the hospital) so make a quick trip to the drive-thru.

Saturday 23 August 2014
Swansea City v Burnley

Of the three Welsh teams that play in the English league (Cardiff, Swansea and Wrexham), Swansea are my second favourite (or second most hated, depends how you look at it). I don't mind Wrexham because we won there 6-2 in 1991 and they are geographically further north. I can't stand Cardiff.

Back in 1991/92 we were coming into spring and had a tough Tuesday night home match against the Bluebirds. A night match at Turf Moor is special, even when the nights are getting lighter and the floodlights aren't turned on until the second half. Those huge magnificent pylon floodlights; they don't make them like that anymore. They don't need to of course, the technology has moved on.

I always think we're going to win night matches. Most of the time anyway. And we usually do. The away game at Ninian Park that season had finished 0-0 but was mostly remembered for the Cardiff fans getting all native and Welsh about things and lobbing bricks into the Burnley end and trying to smash up Burnley cars and buses. It had been in all the local papers. It made me both fear and hate Cardiff at the same time.

The atmosphere before the return match at Turf Moor was different, you could sense something in the air. A tension. I could feel it even though I was still only ten years old. Coming out of the newsagent's on Tod Road with my bag of midget gems, a Burnley fan ran past the shop and shouted at a couple of others (not at me, I wouldn't have been that useful), 'Come on, there's a feight [fight] at Fulledge.' He was beaming as he said this, excited. The others ran after him to join in the fun.

Fulledge Rec was a piece of grassland close to Turf Moor often used for car parking on a matchday. It was only a few hundred yards from where I'd just bought my midget gems. Even though I knew I wasn't going anywhere near to Fulledge, I felt a rush of excitement, not fear. I wanted

Burnley to win. I always do. Fulledge Rec. Turf Moor. Anywhere and everywhere.

Cardiff got what was coming to them, on the pitch at least anyway. Right in front of the Cricket Field End, Robbie Painter gave Burnley the lead after only 16 seconds, which is still the quickest goal I've seen scored by a Burnley player. We went on to win 3-1.

I didn't see any crowd trouble anywhere, but I hoped we had won that too.

The last time we were in the Premier League in 2009/10 our away form was shocking. We drew one, won one, and lost the other 17 away games. I think it's a Premier League record for the most away defeats in one season. And not one we're proud of.

It's going to be different this time though. We've got Dyche in charge.

We lose 1-0 at Swansea.

Oh well, on to the next one. One game at a time. That's the mantra.

Tuesday 26 August 2014
Burnley v Sheff Weds

I'd forgotten about this. I've been too busy looking at our Premier League fixtures so it had sort of escaped me that we're playing in the League Cup tonight against Sheffield Wednesday.

Wednesday themselves were Premier League for a long time before getting relegated in 2000, and then, very much like Man City and Leeds before them, somehow at one point found themselves dropping to the third tier. They're back in the Championship now but never really look like they're going to get out of it at the end they'd like to. I still can't believe they didn't knock down that stand and rebuild something nice in its place. Maybe they'll get promoted once they've done that.

Anyway, I'm not normally that bothered about the League Cup, especially the early rounds. But, actually, this might be good for us, get a nice win under our belts, to give us a lift. Obviously Sean will make a few changes because it's only Wednesday and we're in the Prem (Prem – that's what you call the Premier League when you're in it) and they're not, but yes, a nice healthy result would be just the job.

We get beat 1-0.

Oh well, it's only the League Cup.

I've had worse matches against Wednesday. An early kick-off on New Year's Eve 2005 against a team from Yorkshire sounded like a recipe for trouble. It was. For me at least anyway.

I started the day in one world and I left it in another, in a no man's land that scared me to death.

The 1pm kick-off time had meant there was limited time for drinking before the game, but more afterwards. The game was irrelevant, we got beat 2-1; I was a bit pissed off, but I don't think that had any bearing on the fact that later that day I put my essential possessions into bin bags and walked out on my wife of five months, who was expecting my baby.

I spent the evening in the Coaching House pub with my Uncle Tony pouring pint after pint of lager down my neck to make the pain go away. I had to numb the enormity of what I had just done, because I knew that the horse had bolted and there was no going back.

The night turned cold and the footpaths icy. I lost count of the number of times I fell over on the short walk home. The walk back to my mum and dad's house. Stumbling in with holes in both the knees of my jeans and matching blobs of red peeking through. A dark, dark day. Far darker than anything I've had this year. Cancer has been a doddle compared to that.

Friday 29 August 2014

Save for a scan, which they've told me to wait a few weeks for, I am done. I'll be back at work soon enough, but not before I get over to a Burnley game, my first since that game against Forest in February. A lifetime ago.

I fly Friday morning with the intention of spending the day with George but it doesn't work out. He has his own life.

My dad thinks that I need to go for a walk with him and his mate and then to the pub. He does this a lot – combines health and vice – all those pints don't really count because he walks to the pub. Clever. It sounds like a great idea. I don't know whether he is trying to prove that I am well, or whether I am trying to show him that I am, but it's a stern test. We walk about ten miles over terrain that is unnatural to walk on, rocky, hilly, bleak pissing rain. Who the fuck designed the Yorkshire Dales? What were they thinking? I manage it. I feel grand. I am gagging for a few pints.

Saturday 30 August 2014
Burnley v Manchester United

The home match against Stoke in January 2007 felt like the end of something for me. It was a strange match. I can't remember the reasons why but the away end was closed for the night, so the Stoke fans had been given the Jimmy Mc Lower and we'd been relocated, just for one match, to the Longside lower. We'd been static for a few seasons as fans had got bored of the football under Cotterill. That night against Stoke our group of ten season ticket holders from a couple of seasons ago was reduced to just me and our Jim.

Right from the start the game had 0-0 written all over it as neither team looked like they had any intention of doing anything. Miraculously, though, midway through the first half, Stoke got a very fortunate goal to put them 1-0 up. The rest of the half was the same again. Dull. The crowd, not a bad one by number, was quiet. And fed up.

Me and Jim got a couple of pints down us with a couple of Bene 'n' hot chasers and checked the odds at the in-ground betting terminal. Bizarrely, Burnley to win 2-1 was as short as 4/1. Stoke to win 1-0 was 10/1. We figured that it was highly likely that there would not be another goal in this game. How there had even been one already was a mystery, but miracles can't happen again.

We ummed and ahhed, but went for it and split a £20 bet on Stoke to win 1-0.

Of course, we were both £100 up by the end of the match, as, as we'd expected, nobody came within an inch of a goal during the second half.

I was down in other ways though. For the first time ever I had bet against Burnley. Okay, you could argue that all I had done was bet on the second half being goalless as Stoke were already 1-0 up when we made the bet. But still, I didn't even care that we got beat. That was something I hadn't experienced before – I was apathetic about it.

At Christmas just a few weeks earlier I'd already decided that I was moving to Northern Ireland, for a year or two anyway. I do sometimes wonder, had Burnley not been so dreadful and depressing to watch around that time, what would have happened? Would I have moved away? If I hadn't would Sam and Oscar have been born? Who knows, maybe I should be grateful for Cotterball.

I'm back at the Turf for the first time since that magical display against Nottingham Forest. The thought I'd never step foot in Turf Moor again never crossed my mind, not even for a minute. We're playing Man United which is as good as it gets.

Back in the 2009/10 season under Coyle we'd played Man United in the first home game. Michael Carrick missed a penalty and Robbie Blake scored a cracker to give us a 1-0 win. It was one of those typical Roy of the Rovers-style wins that we got under Coyle.

Today, we're different though. It's more hard work and getting what we deserve than romantic flukes built on the lies of a Judas.

We get a deserved point in a 0-0 draw.

I have a few pints in the Rising Sun with Carl late on Saturday. He's come back from the Wolves game (they've beaten the Bastards 3-1 at Molineux – good lads Wolves) so it's past 9pm before he gets there. We stay until closing. He can't believe how well I look, and how I've recovered so quickly. He's impressed that I've been drinking for 12 hours. So am I. I feel invincible. I'm a fucking warrior.

He's no fuel left in his car so I tell him I'll walk back down the hill to my mum and dad's house. It's only a mile away, but the night is getting cold. I 'inherit' another Wolves item, this time a hoodie, pull it on over the top of my Burnley shirt, and set off on my way. The first half mile is gradually uphill and is well lit with street lights. The last half mile is pretty much all steep downhill, but, and I'd forgotten this, there are no lights. It's pitch black. I can't work out whether I want cars to drive down here or not. I could use the lights to see where I'm going. But the downside is that they may well mow me down. The torch function on this Blackberry is non-existent, especially when I've run out of charge. I don't see any cars. At one point I almost trip over something. It's an animal, I can't make out what … probably a fox. I survive though. So does the fox – he's lucky that he's not a sheep and I'm not a Leeds fan.

Sunday 31 August 2014

I wake up in Blacko needing a piss. I have one.

Five hours later I'm back in Bangor. I still need a piss. And another, and another. I can go. A bit. But not all the time. And not a lot. What is this?

We go out for lunch to the Jamaica Inn. I get a pint of Guinness. I drink only three-quarters of it. I'm not right. We get home and I take my temperature. It's sky high. I can't ring the McDermott Unit because it's Sunday and they're closed so I phone the emergency number on my chemo poster. They tell me to get to A&E asap. This time I'll have to go there. I know I can't wait for the McDermott Unit to open tomorrow morning.

Catherine parks the car whilst I check myself into A&E. I tell the girl on the reception that I'm a chemotherapy patient.

'Who is a chemotherapy patient?' she asks.

'Me,' I tell her.

I don't look like one, certainly not anymore. I've even got a good bit of hair on my head these days. When she realises what I'm telling her the NHS fast lane appears again and it's straight through into Triage. It's like being in the FBI, 'Federal agent coming through'. I wave my chemo badge at them and they all step aside and let me pass. It gets me Rolls-Royce treatment as far as the NHS is concerned.

They give me antibiotics for a suspected urinary tract infection (UTI). It reminds me of Tom Hanks in *The Green Mile*. They take urine samples – it's like pissing razor blades (Hanks' character said that – I now know what he means – I should watch that film again and feel a new level of connection) and it takes me a while to get them anything.

My temperature is crazy high. They keep checking it. They tell me to drink plenty of fluids and put me on a drip to make sure. They try some different antibiotics. It feels random. They don't seem to know what to give me.

It gets to about 10pm and I realise I'm not getting home tonight. They take me to the ward. There are six beds together, it's dark and nobody is about. They've got me on a drip pumping water into me slowly. All about getting fluids in, they keep saying to me. They encourage me to sleep.

But it is torture. I'm baking hot and not only am I needing to drink a lot of water, I have this fluid being squirted into me. I'm then needing to piss. Taking this bastard thing with me is a complete pain in the arse. I think about the McDermott Unit and how I never bothered going to the toilet because it was too much hassle, just like an aeroplane. That chemo shit was easy compared to this. I go to all that effort and when I get there, nothing. So frustrating.

I don't know when but I eventually get to sleep.

Monday 1 September 2014

I wake up to the sound of laughter. My eyes are still closed but I'm awake. It's daytime, I can feel the sun through my eyes. It's noisy. The laughter is different people. It's near me, then it disappears. Not gradually. Then it starts again. It's only near me. It's not distant. The laugh is on me.

I'm lying on top of the bed sheets rather than under them. They're laughing at me. Am I completely naked? Is that what's so funny?

Well it had been a warm night, and this temperature of mine isn't doing so good. I put my hand towards my groin and am delighted to find I've kept my boxers on. Well done me. Get the lad a pint. Or maybe don't, that might be the problem.

I open my eyes. I'm surrounded by old timers. There are two rows of three beds, I'm on the end near the open corridor. The old guy across from me is a particularly disgusting character.

A nurse walks past me and says, 'Good morning Brian.' I can't work out who she's talking to.

It's only a bit later on when another nurse comes right over to the side of my bed with a trolley and says, 'Hi Brian, can I do some obs?' that I realise they think I'm called Brian.

'I'm not called Brian,' I tell her.

'Oh,' she replies, 'well why do they call you Brian, is that your middle name?'

No, I shake my head. I'm nothing to do with Brian. I tell her my name is Michael as she goes about her business.

'Well then Michael,' she says, 'you are hot stuff.'

She's referencing the temperature reading she's just taken from my ear whilst at the same time flirting with me in that awkward way that middle-aged women can do. It makes me shy and embarrassed. She tells me I'm over 105. I've enough kids to know that that is hot – because what you do these days with kids is check their temperature all the time with a proper thermometer – but not enough medical experience to realise how hot. She's not seen a temperature this high in the last 15 years. I get off on being a record breaker. Take what comes to you.

Word has reached Dr Ong of my ailment. I know this because unexpectedly she appears right next to me. I nearly shit myself. She talks about low immunity and neutropaenia making me susceptible to infection. She asks whether I've been taking it easy. Rather than mention the plane journey, the football match, the ten-mile walk in the rain or the walk back from the pub at midnight, or the 20 or so pints I've had at the weekend, I simply offer her a 'maybe I've been overdoing it'.

She starts a mini lecture but she gets distracted – she's busy negotiating my release. Bad news is I'm not going home yet. The good news is that she's taking me down to the haematology ward ('my ward' as she calls it) and getting me my own room.

That's a relief; not only will I get my own space but I won't have to look at the old timer across from me – I can't work out what is going on with his pyjama bottoms but he has his ball bag on full display. I think it's connected to the bag of piss he carries around with him. I'm admiring the view of the old timer when I spot a piece of paper on the wall above his bed. On it, in black marker, it reads WILLIAM. I slowly turn around to have a look at the wall behind me. I have a similar piece of paper above my bed, which, sure enough, says BRIAN. When another nurse stops by to do some obs (they're doing these about every half hour) I point out that I'm not called Brian. She looks at me, looks at the sign and asks, 'Why does it say Brian on there then?'

That is a very good question.

Flirty middle-aged nurse is back to give me some medication. She asks about my family and all that and whether I'd want to have any more kids. She's potentially offering to carry my babies but I ignore that and tell her that it's unlikely I'll be able to have any more children because of my chemotherapy treatment. She looks at me like I'm talking in Russian.

'What?' she demands. 'A big lad like you … a big strapping lad like you … you'll be fine.'

I don't believe her, but she convinces me that in a few weeks' time I should get a test done to check. I'll hold that thought.

Shortly before my transfer my wife arrives with the boys and some extra clothes and things for me. It really is no place for kids. They're running around like maniacs and getting too near the bloke across from me. I shout for them to come back.

'They're okay, the chap doesn't seem to mind,' Catherine tells me.

'I'm worried that they're going to knock over his bag of piss,' I reply as though it's an everyday hazard. Oh, what has it come to?

Sunday 7 September 2014

Well that was a week of sheer frustration. I'd started to feel better from Monday afternoon onwards and near enough fine from Tuesday. But because of this bloody cancer thing they're being ultra-cautious. They want to keep assessing me, observing me, checking my temperature, giving me fluids, antibiotics. You can fake a lot of things but temperature isn't one of them and it took a while to settle down to a consistent normal level.

It was the boredom that got me. I was stuck in the same room for the full week practically, but feeling completely fine (for most of it). I only left the room to have a shower. I ate every meal in the same room. And the food. Well it wasn't that bad at first but it's the monotony of it. I'd worked out though that the chicken was good. The mash was that sort of hard tinned mash that you can't believe exists and it was awful. But the chicken gravy was actually reasonably nice so if you 'caught it' in time you could use it to massively lift the mash. I say 'caught it'. On more than one occasion the food arrived whilst I was having something done (like medical type stuff, I've no idea, I lose track). The gravy, if left to its own devices, would solidify into a gloop, and I'd need to work hard to agitate it back to gravy. It's work, just of a different nature.

Getting out of hospital is not easy. Especially at the weekend. There is risk aversion everywhere, no one wants to make the call. And when they do there's the paperwork. I don't know what they mean, can they not just find my 'papers' and scrawl on the front page 'he's fucked off' or even just 'gone' would work.

By the time Dickens had written whatever needed to be written I walked out of the building. Catherine hadn't yet arrived to collect me so I was still going nowhere, but I couldn't wait any longer. I walked out into that fresh late-summer air and felt free. Free from the hospital, free from cancer. But sure I was free a week ago? This felt different though, properly free, I have properly done this. I've had a bit of a wobble, I've got to neutropaenia, I know what that looks like, I've bought the T-shirt, and I've handled it, and now that's done, and I've properly done it.

Now for the real business. I've a football team to sort out. Oh, and a real job to go back to. Can't forget about that one in all this excitement.

Saturday 20 September 2014

I'm excited to watch my team play for the first time. Even Mourinho had to start somewhere.

He probably didn't start with a 15-0 defeat though. Not that they'll publish the score. It was hard to watch. We ship a couple of early goals and it gradually gets worse – and worse. The opposition ask us if we want to throw an extra player on. Or two? How about three?

I go from praying we can get ourselves a foothold in the game to praying that our kids don't have the ability to count.

Oh well. It can't get much worse. Onwards and upwards.

Part Five

TODAY AGAIN

Saturday 21 February 2015

I bounce into the house wet through, and for the second time in the space of a couple of hours I have a tale of victory to tell. I just knew it. I couldn't lose today. It wouldn't be fair. You see me and God, we do these deals. He gave me cancer with one hand. He got me promoted with the other. There is some strange kind of fairness to it.

I tell you what then God, while we're at it, go get me a result today at Chelsea. We're sat 18th in the Premier League, in the relegation zone. Where everybody thought we would be, but go on, today, get me something.

Chelsea take the lead early on through Ivanovic and I'm wondering whether the big guy was listening to me after all. It all changes on 71 minutes. Matic sees red following his reaction to a tackle by Ashley Barnes, and with less than ten minutes to go Ben Mee pops up for the equaliser. We take a point from the team top of the league and look set to secure the title.

I watch *Match of the Day* with more attention when I like the content. I watch it more than once tonight. Mourinho is raging. Dyche oozes class. What a man.

Part Six

TOMORROW

Tuesday 6 February 2018

It's anniversary season for me. Not wedding. Not birthday. It's my markers. My events. Memorable days and dates that are etched on my mind forever. The days that shook me up and slapped me about like never before. So now measure me. I'm better than I was four years ago.

It's a Tuesday. I like a Tuesday morning. I look after myself and Catherine sorts all the kids. All three of them now that is.

The car radio tells me it's World Cancer Day today. A quick google when I get to work informs me that it's always World Cancer Day on 6 February, even in 2014. You have to laugh at the irony of that one. It's meant to be an awareness day, not the day when they shout 'Surprise!' to you in the morning when you're about to have a shave.

I live a completely normal life.

I have a scar on my neck from the biopsy, it's only about an inch long, and you'd never even know it's there as it's right on a natural crease in my neck. Mr Ullah did a good job with it. I didn't know before but Mr is better than Dr!

Every morning, without fail, before I even open my eyes, I feel my neck to check for lumps. It takes about two seconds and I do it on auto pilot. Each day when I feel nothing I get a mini boost. It's a great way to start the day – hip hip hooray, today I don't have cancer.

I'm not cured. They won't let me have that status for five years. But I am in what they call full remission, so I'm as cured as I can be. There must be a partial remission. I don't know much about that. Which part? I don't get that. Even that word remission. I had that down as a naughty word as well. I didn't know what it meant but if you'd told me somebody was in remission I'd have thought they were 50:50 dying or not.

Do I need to wait five years to reflect? Do I bollocks. Five years is a government statistic based on history and probability. It's nothing to do with me. I could get this again at any given moment, one year, two years, five years, ten years or 20 years. Anybody could. Or alternatively, and preferably, never.

Am I jinxing it in some way by reflecting? No. Or maybe? Who knows? Quite what I did to jinx it last time I have no idea. Seriously. What did I do? Did I swear too much? I hope not. If that's it I'm truly fucked.

It will be what it will be, won't it? If it comes again, or one of its ugly mates, I'll be ready and waiting to go toe to toe again. I know the score. I've won the World Cup once, I can do it again.

I don't take any medication. I have paracetamol quite a lot when I'm hungover, but these aren't prescribed to me. They're just from Tesco. Again, this is not what I thought it would be like. I was convinced that one way or another they'd be shooting me up with shit forever.

Do I watch what I eat and drink? I do yes, but only because I don't eat with my eyes closed, apart from kebabs when I'm pissed. I don't take note and count anything. I don't know what a calorie is. I know what a unit of alcohol is but I'm in denial about that. My glass bin is well used. But at least I'm recycling.

I'm definitely in part two though. I am. I feel it.

Part one ended on 21 February 2014. Part two started on 22 February, the day we beat Nottingham Forest.

I'm not different. But I am a bit. I feel it. A bit. I hate detail and am much more big picture than I was. I'm slightly more socialist. I feel like I'm more part of the world than I was before. Like I'm in the melting pot with everybody else.

Before that, I thought that stuff like cancer was for other people. Not me. I was in the top sets at school, the football team, I got my 2:1 degree from a good university, got a good job, became a chartered accountant, chartered tax adviser, got married (twice, a few road bumps around that but I came out of it okay), nice house, three kids. It's been a pretty easy life to be honest. It all somehow works out for me. And the cancer and other bad stuff, well, that's for the unlucky ones.

But then 21 February 2014 came. And I learnt that was all fucking bullshit. It doesn't discriminate. It can happen to anybody at any time. And I'm just like everybody else. And I need other people. I need nurses; do I need those angels. And I need friends. And I need to do stuff for other people. Nice stuff. I am different. I've heard your 33rd year referred to as your 'Jesus year', I think because that's when we think he was arrested and crucified. The Urban Dictionary defines it as 'The 33rd year of your life where you are reborn in some sense'. It's scary because that's exactly what I feel like.

Strange how things happen. I did what the nurse told me to. I took a fertility test in October 2014. Yep, I was a dud. A jaffa. Seedless. She was wrong. She said a big lad like me would be okay. It's not all bad, I thought. It saves me having a vasectomy – think of the positives. We didn't even know if we wanted more kids and at least it saves us having to make a decision. It just wasn't meant to be.

Well, actually, it was. And the nurse I just said was wrong, well she was right. It's crazy how the human body can replace and renew. Just like my hair came back, so did my fertility. I couldn't put a date on it because they (the boys down there) can't speak to tell me, but Finn was born on 17 November 2015, so probably sometime in February 2015. Probably 21 February 2015, I seem to have a thing for that day. How that all works I've no idea, and perhaps the doctor who gave me the test results saying I had a zero count should have caveated it a bit more. But when she told me she was pregnant, aside from complete shock, I felt a huge sense of pride. It's not the being fertile, it's the bouncing back from not being. The fucking comeback king. I'm fucking invincible. I love that underdog Dunkirk thing.

It's just like the Clarets. We were duly relegated from the Premier League in May 2015. But we bounced back, winning the Championship the following May. No messing. Bang. We managed to stay up last season, and right now we're sat seventh in the Premier League. Yes, seventh. Carry on like this and we'll be qualifying for Europe, lol lol. A pub in Burnley near the Turf has even said they'll rename the pub after Dyche if we make it. Looking back a few more years, my whole Burnley supporting life since 1987 has been one massive comeback.

Progression. Upwards trajectories. I love them. Take Kieran Trippier. Great player he was in that game against Forest in 2014 he was getting a reputation as a piss head. The lad's just made his England debut and he's a decent chance of being in the England squad for the World Cup in Russia. That's a measure.

I honestly don't know whether Finn would have been born had I not had cancer. Probably not. But a lot of things would be different. I probably wouldn't have kick-started my football 'career' without the cancer.

And things would be even more different had I not had football. I don't know how I would have coped with cancer. What would I have done to take my mind away? Where would

I find my attitude and my role model? Not in a cancer survival guide, that's for sure. Finn is as much to do with football as he is cancer. More so in fact. All my most meaningful relationships are rooted in football. It makes people my friend (in fact, to be fair I think men who don't like football are oddballs and I keep my distance from them). It's my connection to my family, to my grandad, my dad, my brother, my uncle, to George. And to my NI boys who are helping me build our own claret-and-blue corner of County Down.

And when I got sick, and fair enough I have to concede that I was, on paper at least, sick, I needed football more than ever. It was there for me, just like it always has been. That first 45 minutes against Nottingham Forest was unbelievable. It was from another planet. It was like the football gods were sorting me out. And then Dyche, he kept going on about the 'one game at a time mantra', 'not overthinking it' and being 'relentless', and I was thinking 'holy shit does he realise he's speaking to me?' And when the season finished I knew that I couldn't be without football. I had to keep it going somehow.

I had a conversation with a work colleague a few months ago. My colleague's elderly mother has just been diagnosed with a form of blood cancer and is undergoing treatment, under the care of the very same Dr Ong. Naturally, my colleague wanted to talk with me about the impact that my treatment had on me.

'Michael, your chemotherapy didn't seem to affect you much.'

'Well, no not really, I felt fine.'

'Did you have to change much in terms of things you did?'

'No, nothing.'

'Well what about your football coaching, did you have to stop that for a period of time?'

My colleague's recollection was wrong of course, or perhaps she didn't know me as well a few years ago, and didn't realise that the football coaching came after and largely because of the cancer. Before the cancer I was football idle.

So my answer to her question was easy.

'No, I didn't have to stop … I had to start.'

And it's true. I had to. I didn't have a choice in the matter. Not really.

Football.

Life.

Death.

Fuck.